Semi-Supervised Learning and Domain Adaptation in Natural Language Processing

Synthesis Lectures on Human Language Technologies

Editor
Graeme Hirst, *University of Toronto*

Synthesis Lectures on Human Language Technologies is edited by Graeme Hirst of the University of Toronto. The series consists of 50- to 150-page monographs on topics relating to natural language processing, computational linguistics, information retrieval, and spoken language understanding. Emphasis is on important new techniques, on new applications, and on topics that combine two or more HLT subfields.

Introduction to Chinese Natural Language Processing
Kam-Fai Wong, Wenjie Li, Ruifeng Xu, and Zheng-sheng Zhang
2009

Introduction to Linguistic Annotation and Text Analytics
Graham Wilcock
2009

Dependency Parsing
Sandra Kübler, Ryan McDonald, and Joakim Nivre
2009

Statistical Language Models for Information Retrieval
ChengXiang Zhai
2008

Semi-Supervised Learning and Domain Adaptation in Natural Language Processing
Anders Søgaard

ISBN: 978-3-031-01021-7   paperback
ISBN: 978-3-031-02149-7   ebook

DOI 10.1007/978-3-031-02149-7

A Publication in the Morgan & Claypool Publishers series
SYNTHESIS LECTURES ON HUMAN LANGUAGE TECHNOLOGIES
Lecture #21
Series Editor: Graeme Hirst, University of Toronto
Series ISSN
Synthesis Lectures on Human Language Technologies
Print 1947-4040 Electronic 1947-4059

Semi-Supervised Learning and Domain Adaptation in Natural Language Processing

Anders Søgaard
University of Copenhagen

SYNTHESIS LECTURES ON HUMAN LANGUAGE TECHNOLOGIES #21

ABSTRACT

This book introduces basic supervised learning algorithms applicable to natural language processing (NLP) and shows how the performance of these algorithms can often be improved by exploiting the marginal distribution of large amounts of unlabeled data. One reason for that is data sparsity, i.e., the limited amounts of data we have available in NLP. However, in most real-world NLP applications our labeled data is also heavily biased. This book introduces extensions of supervised learning algorithms to cope with data sparsity and different kinds of sampling bias.

This book is intended to be *both* readable by first-year students *and* interesting to the expert audience. My intention was to introduce what is necessary to appreciate the major challenges we face in contemporary NLP related to data sparsity and sampling bias, without wasting too much time on details about supervised learning algorithms or particular NLP applications. I use text classification, part-of-speech tagging, and dependency parsing as running examples, and limit myself to a small set of cardinal learning algorithms. I have worried less about theoretical guarantees ("this algorithm never does too badly") than about useful rules of thumb ("in this case this algorithm may perform really well"). In NLP, data is so noisy, biased, and non-stationary that few theoretical guarantees can be established and we are typically left with our gut feelings and a catalogue of crazy ideas. I hope this book will provide its readers with both. Throughout the book we include snippets of Python code and empirical evaluations, when relevant.

KEYWORDS

natural language processing, machine learning, learning under bias, semi-supervised learning

Contents

CHAPTER 1

Introduction

1.1 INTRODUCTION

In natural language processing (NLP), we are interested in language at many different levels. In multi-document summarization, we are concerned with collections of documents; if we want to build a spam filter, we are concerned with single emails; in constituent-based parsing, we learn to combine phrases; in dependency parsing, we predict syntactic dependencies between pairs of words; in word sense disambiguation, we find the correct sense for each word in context. In order to learn how to summarize, classify documents, parse sentences, or disambiguate words, we need to be able to represent language in a compact, meaningful way. In NLP, we represent language (documents, sentences, words) by arrays of numbers, most often 0s and 1s.

$$\langle 0, 1, 0, 0, 1 \rangle$$

could, for example, represent the text:

McCain just gave a cheap plug to Ed Kennedy.

The array may be a series of values for the attributes $\langle$Obama, McCain, Malcolm X, Mary Poppins, Ed Kennedy$\rangle$, where 1 means that a feature (word) is present in the text and 0 means it isn't. This way of representing text is known as the *bag-of-words* model. If a text can be represented as an array of numerical values, we can represent a collection of documents as a 2-dimensional array or as a matrix with data points as rows.

Say some of the rows in a matrix are of particular interest to us. The above sentence was posted on Twitter under the 2008 debates. Say we have a sample of tweets, and we want to identify those written by Republicans, those written by women, or those in which the word *plug* is used in a particular sense. Instead of manually sorting the tweets, we hand-label a small sample of them and train a classifier to automatically sort the rest of them. Each data point $\mathbf{x} = x_1 \ldots x_m$ in our labeled sample is then provided a label:

$$\langle 1, \langle 0, 1, 0, 0, 1 \rangle \rangle \text{ or, in sparse format: } \langle 1, \langle 1 : 1, 4 : 1 \rangle \rangle$$

We write $\mathbf{x}$ for data points and y for class labels. Every feature $x_i \in \mathbf{x}$ is called an observed variable; labels are values of *output* variables. In structure prediction, data points are associated with several output variables, but, in classification, a labeled data point consists of observed variables and a single output variable. For now, output variables are assumed to be binary, i.e., with labels $y \in \{0, 1\}$, but, the observed variables can be both discrete (with values 0 and 1) and continuous (real-valued). Note that we can visualize data points with n observed variables in n-dimensional space. Say we represent texts by the frequency of the words *McCain* and *Obama*. The above text would then be represented by the array $\langle .2, 0 \rangle$. In the same way, Figure 1.1 is a Pylab plot of 111 positive and 111 negative movie user reviews from the IMDb[1] dataset used in Maas et al. [81] by the frequencies of the words "love" (horizontal axis) and "boring" (vertical axis). Note that the diagonal $f(x) \geq x$ discriminates positives from negatives fairly well. Everything above the line is a negative data point, and most of the data points below it are positives. Such discriminants will be referred to as *decision boundaries*. Supervised learning algorithms use small hand-labeled samples of data to learn decision boundaries that discriminate between classes in data.

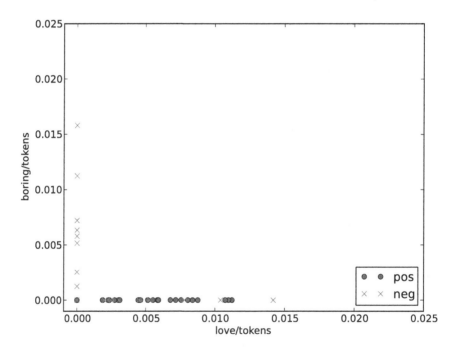

Figure 1.1: IMDb user reviews by keyword frequencies (toy example).

Chapter 2 introduces a handful of learning algorithms for classifying new data points, e.g., tweets or user reviews, from hand-labeled data, as well as a couple of clustering algorithms for finding natural clusters in data without relying on hand-labeled data. However, while classification and clustering algorithms find massive applications in NLP, classification or clustering is, typically,

[1]http://www.imdb.com/

not the end goal in NLP. Here we are typically interested in *linguistic structures*. Think of dependency parsing (see Section 2.9), for example. In dependency parsing, we want to predict a syntactic analysis, such as the one in Figure 1.2 for an input sentence. If we think of trees as classes, the number of classes would be enormous. Even if we restrict ourselves to looking at sentences with 17 tokens, and only consider *unlabeled* trees without annotation of grammatical functions, the number of classes would be $17^{15} \sim 3 \times 10^{18}$ (by Cayley's formula). So, in other words, we somehow have to break down the prediction problem into smaller units. On the other hand, if we simply think of parsing as a series of mutually independent classifications—for example, what is the most likely syntactic head for each word?—we do not model the intricate dependencies between these smaller units, and performance will be poor. The answer is to combine classification or clustering algorithms with search or parsing algorithms. The move to structure prediction from classification and clustering is taken in Sections 2.8 and 2.9.

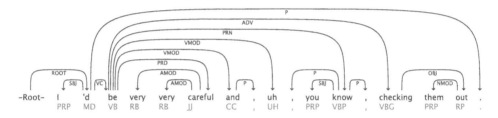

Figure 1.2: Syntactic analysis (Switchboard Corpus). Directed edges represent grammatical functions, from syntactic heads to their dependents.

Chapter 2 thus covers basic topics in NLP and can probably be skipped by an expert audience. The remaining four chapters introduce less commonly taught topics related to semi-supervised learning and domain adaptation. This focus is motivated in the next section.

1.2   LEARNING UNDER BIAS

In most real-world applications of supervised document classification, the labeled data available is scarce and biased. This holds for other real-world learning problems too. Samples in medical studies are typically not representative of the general population. Object recognition typically relies on product pictures from services such as Amazon,[2] but, users may apply object recognition technology to holiday snapshots or security cam frames. Nevertheless, NLP sometimes seems particularly vulnerable. In most machine learning datasets with n data points and m features, $n > m$ by a large margin. In NLP it is most often the other way around. The fact that our labeled data is so sparse makes us more vulnerable to data bias.

---

[2]http://www.amazon.com/

In spam filtering, spam detection models usually are acquired from contributed emails or from the Enron corpus.[3] Such datasets are heavily biased in multiple ways, containing only emails written by computer scientists or former Enron employees about work-related matters, and are already several years old. Sites such as IMDb and Amazon give us labeled data for polarity detection, but only for a limited set of categories. If we want to apply our models to new types of products, our results are influenced by what we may think of as a sampling bias. In part-of-speech (POS) tagging and dependency parsing, the most widely used dataset is The Wall Street Journal section of the Penn Treebank [84]. However, unless we are only interested in parsing (late 1980s) The Wall Street Journal our induced models will be heavily biased when applied to real-world data.

So, what can we do? In supervised learning, we have our data, a feature representation, e.g., a bag-of-words model, and a preferred algorithm that learns a model (a set of parameters). Such algorithms will be introduced in Chapter 2. If we want to do better than just ignoring the bias, we can do three things:

(a) Replace our preferred algorithm with an algorithm that *underfits* data, for example, that only learns relatively simple, superficial correlations from data, believed to be common to the available data (the *source* data) and the data we wish to process (the *target* data).

(b) Use semi-supervised learning to learn from labeled source and unlabeled target domain data. Semi-supervised learning algorithms are introduced in Chapter 3. Briefly put, these algorithms use the distributional properties of large samples of unlabeled data to complement the knowledge that is obtained from the available labeled data.

(c) Use only some of the data, some of the features, or some of the model parameters in the target data. The idea is that some data points, features, or model parameters will be specific to the source data, and we may adapt to the target data—or correct the data bias—by simply letting go of these data points, features, or parameters.

Option (a) is not particularly attractive, but may, in some cases, lead to small improvements over a fully optimized supervised baseline (which assumes target data looks exactly like the source data; see Section 2.1 for more on the assumptions of supervised learning algorithms). Option (b) is probably the most common way of approaching the data bias problem; we consider semi-supervised learning for learning under bias in Chapter 3. Option (c) is discussed in Chapter 4, where we present algorithms specifically designed for *learning under bias*.[4]

The algorithms covered in Chapter 4, however, rely on the target domain being known. In many NLP applications, that is not the case. When we design publicly available tools such as POS taggers or syntactic parsers, we do not know in advance what data end users will feed to our systems.

---

[3]http://www.cs.cmu.edu/~enron/

[4]In NLP, the most common term for the data bias problem is *domain adaptation* (which is why it is in the title of this book). In machine learning, the more common term is *transfer learning*. Since the methods discussed in this book apply to more than bias caused by domain shifts and include methods not intuitively about transfer, we will often use the more inclusive term of *learning under bias*.

When we develop online services such as translation services or online sentiment analysis, we do not know what data our system will be fed by end users in advance. This problem is addressed in Chapter 5. Finally, Chapter 6 discusses challenges in evaluating NLP systems when we assume that the available labeled data is almost always severely biased.

Inductive Bias and Bias in Data

⑤[5] The word "bias" has several usages in machine learning and NLP. When we speak of bias-variance trade-off in Chapter 2, for example, we speak of the bias of a learning algorithm. In this section we talked about bias in data. In the former case bias refers to "any bias for choosing one generalization over another, other than strict consistency with the observed training instances" [92]. In other words, the bias of a learning algorithm is the assumptions it makes about the learned model *a priori*. This bias is often called *inductive bias*. Bias in data, on the other hand, refers to a violation of the assumption that data is *identically distributed* (see Section 2.1).

1.3   EMPIRICAL EVALUATIONS

In this book, we will present empirical evaluations of the algorithms discussed, when relevant. Our empirical evaluations focus on three applications, namely document classification, POS tagging, and dependency parsing.

The goal of **document classification** is the automatic assignment of documents into pre-defined semantic classes. Examples of document classification problems include polarity detection, authorship attribution, spam filtering, topic classification, relevance filtering, and adding MeSH terms to Medline abstracts. The input is a set of labeled documents $\langle y_1, \mathbf{x}_1 \rangle, \ldots, \langle y_N, \mathbf{x}_N \rangle$, and the task is to learn a function $f : \mathcal{X} \mapsto \mathcal{Y}$ that is able to correctly classify previously unseen documents. Each data point is a binary or real-valued vector. For empirical evaluations, we will use the 20 Newsgroups dataset.[6] The task here, as the name suggests, is to learn a function from vectors representing Usenet posts into newsgroup labels. Two of these newsgroups are posts related to hockey and baseball. We refer to the problem of distinguishing between posts in these two newsgroups as the Hockey-Baseball problem, which we will use to illustrate strengths and weaknesses of supervised learning algorithms in Chapter 2.

The topics in 20 Newsgroups are hierarchically structured, which enables us to do domain adaptation experiments [25, 132]. See the hierarchy in Figure 1.3. We extract 20 high-level binary classification problems by considering all pairs of top-level categories, e.g., Computers-Recreative (comp-rec). For each of these 20 problems, we have different possible datasets, e.g., IBM-Baseball, Mac-Motorcycles, etc. A *problem instance* takes training and test data from two different datasets belonging to the same high-level problem. For example, a problem instance could be learning to distinguish articles about Macintosh and motorcycles Mac-Motorcycles (evaluated on the 20 Newsgroups test section) using labeled data from IBM-Baseball (the train-

---

[5]In this book we will use the symbol ⑤ when issuing friendly warnings about possible caveats or potentially confusing terminology.
[6]http://people.csail.mit.edu/jrennie/20Newsgroups/

ing section). In total we have 288 available problem instances in the 20 Newsgroups dataset.[7] Most of our evaluations will concern subsets of this set of problem instances, but, we will also present evaluations in POS tagging and dependency parsing, when relevant.

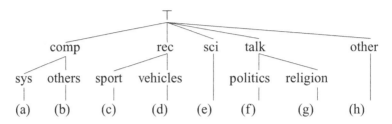

Figure 1.3: Hierarchical structure of 20 Newsgroups. (a) IBM, Mac, (b) Graphics, MS-Windows, X-Windows, (c) Baseball, Hockey, (d) Autos, Motorcycles, (e) Cryptography, Electronics, Medicine, Space, (f) Guns, Mideast, Miscellaneous, (g) Atheism, Christianity, Miscellaneous, (h) Forsale.

Part-of-speech (POS) tagging is a sequence labeling problem. For a natural language sentence $\mathbf{x} : w_1 \ldots w_n$ we want to predict a sequence of syntactic categories $y : p_1 \ldots p_n$ (nouns, verbs, adjectives, etc.) such that token w_i belongs to syntactic category p_i. Note, however, that while each token is assumed to belong to just one syntactic category, a word form can have different parts of speech in different contexts. So, we observe ambiguities such as "Time/N flies/V like/ADV an/DET arrow/N" vs. "Time/N flies/N like/V an/DET arrow/N." Several tag sets have been proposed by linguists, and while some attempts have been made to bridge targets [103], linguists seem to agree that languages have different sets of parts of speech. For large-scale empirical evaluations of learning algorithms in the context of POS tagging, we use the OntoNotes 4.0 release of The Wall Street Journal section of the Penn Treebank as training data with the various development and test sections of the English Web Treebank.[8] The test sections are sampled from Yahoo! Answers, the Enron email corpus, BBC Newsgroups, local business reviews, and various weblogs. These datasets provide cross-domain learning problems, where the task is learning to tag web data from observing hand-labeled sentences sampled from newspaper material. The email data is reserved for tuning our models and we use the remaining four domains for evaluation.

Dependency parsing is a structure prediction task where the output variables form trees with complex internal structure.[9] Dependency parsing models a sentence as a tree where words are vertices and grammatical functions are directed edges (dependencies). Each word has a single incoming edge, except one called the root of the tree. Thus, dependency parsing is a structure prediction problem

---

[7]There are actually 288×2 datasets, but we do not include instances that only differ by swapping source and target data.
[8]LDC Catalogue No.: LDC2012T13.
[9]Some annotation guidelines and parsers allow for multiple roots. In this case, a dependency structure is a forest of trees. Some annotation guidelines even allow for directed acyclic dependency structures (DAGs) [115], but here we assume that dependency structures are trees.

with trees as structured variables. The problem of classifying configurations into transitions under the arc-standard scheme is used as a toy example in Chapter 2. The training data for this toy example consists of gold configurations from the OntoNotes 4.0 release of the The Wall Street Journal section of the Penn Treebank (annotated data from The Wall Street Journal). The test data consists of the development data from the Emails section of the English Web Treebank. We refer to this dataset as GWEB-EMAIL-TRANSITIONS. For large-scale empirical evaluations of learning algorithms in the context of dependency parsing, we also use the OntoNotes 4.0 release of the The Wall Street Journal section of the Penn Treebank as training data with the various development and test sections of the English Web Treebank.

🛑 In Section 1.1, we talked about observable and output variables. When we learn a function $f : \mathcal{X} \mapsto \mathcal{Y}$, we learn how to induce the values of unobservable output variables from the values of observable ones. In most applications outside NLP, the inferred values of our unobservable variables are predictions about the future that can later be verified by observing the outcome of the variables. In NLP, unobservable variables rarely become observable. Linguistic structures do not reveal themselves over time and cannot be studied in laboratories. They are not observable at all, but are theoretical constructs that remain hidden to us. In most cases, our practical solution is to adopt some linguistic theory and try to predict analyses produced by linguists adhering to that linguistic theory. However, unobservable variables in NLP are moving targets. In syntactic parsing, for example, the correct analysis of a sentence depends very much on your favorite linguistic theory, and linguistic theories evolve, become more or less popular, and are sometimes completely abandoned. In POS tagging, new targets may be introduced. This scenario is sometimes referred to as *concept drift* in the statistical literature [62].

In this book, we use intrinsic evaluation metrics such as accuracy, but it generally makes more sense to do down-stream evaluation of taggers and dependency parsers, which also enables us to compare models across different linguistic theories. This, however, is beyond the scope of this book. Several researchers have discussed parser evaluation recently [61, 93, 94, 145], and we refer the interested reader to their papers. For a related paper on POS tagging, see [82].

CHAPTER 2

Supervised and Unsupervised Prediction

This chapter introduces some common classification and clustering algorithms and discusses how they can be extended to structure prediction problems in NLP. The main focus will be classification. Classification algorithms simply estimate functions $f : \mathcal{X} \mapsto \mathcal{Y}$ from multi-dimensional input space $\mathcal{X}$ to a set of discrete classes $\mathcal{Y}$. Consider, for example, the problem of estimating the polarity of movie reviews—or better, consider *spam filtering*.

The assumption in most spam filters is that spam can be identified in part by looking at the words that occur in emails. Some words are more spam-like than others. Particular words have particular probabilities of occurring in spam email or legitimate email. Say, for every word w, we compute its relative frequency in spam email and legitimate email. Based on these frequencies we decide whether w is evidence for spam or not. A simple classification algorithm could, for example, just count the number of words in any unseen email that are evidence for classifying the email as spam, and if, say, 20 such words are observed, classify the email as spam.

Our data points (representations of emails) in $\mathcal{X}$ could, in this case, just be binary vectors encoding the presence of words in the email. Classifying unseen emails represented this way into $\mathcal{Y} = \{\text{spam, non-spam}\}$ would be a binary classification problem. When we introduce supervised learning algorithms, we will use the spam filtering toy dataset in Figure 2.1 as our running example, where we have observations for three emails and want to predict whether the fourth email is spam or not.

y	zebra	viagra	venus
spam	0	1	0
non-spam	1	0	0
non-spam	1	0	1
?	0	1	1

Figure 2.1: Toy example.

For bigger datasets, we may gather the different classes of documents in separate folders, for example, a folder of spam emails and a folder of non-spam emails. In the code presented throughout the book we will assume that standard Python packages such as numpy, glob, and sys are imported, using the standard abbreviation np for numpy. To turn our documents into vectors, we first need to establish a vocabulary (a set of features). If this is just the words occurring in our documents, we can use `glob` and Python counters to get the vocabulary `wrds`.

```
from collections import Counter as cnt
f1=glob.glob(DIR1+"/*")
f2=glob.glob(DIR2+"/*")
voc=cnt([])
for f in f1+f2:
    wrds+=cnt(open(f).read().split())
```

We can then run through `wrds` to build the individual data points.

```
def found(v,txt):
    return 1 if v in txt else 0
X=[[found(w,open(f).read().lower().split())
    for w in list(dict(wrds).iterkeys())] for f in f1+f2]
```

Alternatively, we can rely on the Python module SkLearn in-built methods to construct our bag-of-words representations.[1] Notice that the in-built methods do implicit tokenization leading to less features than the from-scratch code above.[2]

```
from sklearn.feature_extraction.text import Vectorizer as vec
v=vec()
X=v.fit_transform([open(f).read() for f in f1+f2])
```

We will continue to alternate between from-scratch code and building on top of SkLearn in-built methods below, but we will follow SkLearn conventions throughout the book. The dataset, if printed to a file in tab-separated format, can be read in as follows, working from scratch.

```
def read_data(filename):
    X=[l.strip().split('\t') for l in open(filename).readlines()]
    return array([d[1:] for d in X]), array([d[0] for d in X])
```

A dataset can be encoded this way as a list of lists or as one or two `numpy` arrays. A list of lists X can be converted to an array applying `np.array(X)`. In SkLearn, data is often encoded as sparse matrices, but can be turned back into a `numpy` array by an in-built method called `X.toarray()`. We will typically assume sparse matrices and call the training and test sets `X_train,y_train` and `X_test,y_test`, respectively.

⊙ We have covered how to represent documents as vectors in two pages, but finding good representations in machine learning is an important and non-trivial problem. Using words or unigrams may be reasonable in spam filtering, but in sentiment analysis, for example, a bag-of-words approach is not sufficient. Some words change polarity in the context of negation or comparatives, but we need to go beyond unigrams to model such effects. If we see *good* 50 times and *not good* 50 times in our training data, for example, our model would not associate any polarity with the word *good*.

---

[1] http://scikit-learn.org/

[2] The vectorization also does a tf(t, d) × idf(t, d) transformation of the data. The `text` module also implements a binary bag-of-words model, i.e., `CountVectorizer(binary=True)`.

2.1   STANDARD ASSUMPTIONS IN SUPERVISED LEARNING

Before we get to our first learning algorithms, we discuss some of the standard assumptions in supervised learning. The learning algorithms we discuss in this chapter commit to one or more of these assumptions, and these assumptions are important to understand the empirical results obtained when applying the learning algorithms to different kinds of data.

Smoothness Assumption

The smoothness assumption says that if two data points $\mathbf{x}_i$ and $\mathbf{x}_j$ are close, so should their class labels y_i and y_j be. This is a minimal assumption in order to be able to infer from a finite sample to a possibly infinite set of unseen data points, and it is the only assumption really made by the nearest neighbor classifier, introduced in Section 2.2. In the context of spam filtering, it means we assume that an email that shares many features with known spam emails is likely to be spam.

Independently and Identically Distributed

The second-most important assumption in supervised learning is that data is randomly sampled and independently and identically distributed (i.i.d.). This means that each data point is sampled from the same probability distribution and that all data points are mutually independent. If the roulette ball in a casino lands on *red* 100 times in a row, the next spin is no less likely to be *black*. In the same way, in spam filtering the next email always has the same chance of being a spam email or of containing the word "Viagra."

The i.i.d. assumption simplifies the math in machine learning, but is invalid in most practical learning scenarios [62, 138]. In spam filtering, emails are typically neither independently nor identically distributed. The way email corpora are collected, the occurrence of an email on hockey in an email corpus typically *does* increase the probability of seeing another email on hockey later. This bias, however, is not as alarming as the fact that data is typically not identically distributed, either. Email corpora typically consist of contributed emails, or they are sampled from the Enron corpus. This means that the emails in the training data most likely cover different topics, are written by different authors, and may have different portions of spam than the yet unseen emails we want to classify. These biases affect classification performance. This book is concerned with learning problems where we cannot assume that data is sampled randomly and i.i.d.. Algorithms for automatically correcting bias are introduced in Chapters 3 and 4.

Single Cluster Assumption

Many supervised learning algorithms, but not all, also assume that classes form single, coherent clusters, e.g., Gaussians where instances of a class center around a mean. Nearest neighbor, as already mentioned, does not make this assumption. In the context of spam filtering, this means that both spam and non-spam emails are assumed to form coherent clusters in our feature space. Figure 2.2 illustrates the single cluster assumption using artificial two-dimensional data. The single cluster assumption is also called the *coherence assumption* [148], but is not to be confused with the *cluster*

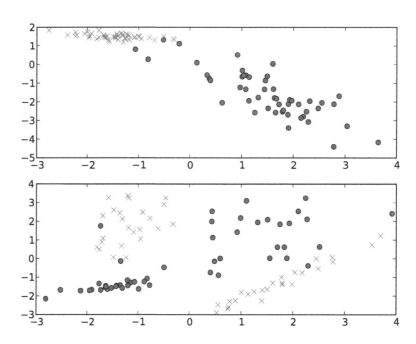

Figure 2.2: Binary classification problems where each class consists of one or two clusters.

assumption [148], which states that two data points in the same cluster are likely to belong to the same class. This latter assumption is essentially the same as what we call the low-density separation assumption.

Low-density Separation

Many learning algorithms assume classes are linearly separable [110, 137], but this assumption can be weakened by assuming only that the best separators lie in low-density regions. Consider the plot in Figure 2.3 for illustration. This assumption is important for many semi-supervised learning algorithms.

2.1.1   HOW TO CHECK WHETHER THE ASSUMPTIONS HOLD

While these assumptions often do not hold in NLP, data may be more or less coherent and more or less separable. Similarly, distributions can be more or less different, and data points can be more or less dependent. This subsection introduces standard metrics that quantify to what extent the i.i.d. assumption, the coherence assumption, and the separability assumption hold. To quantify to

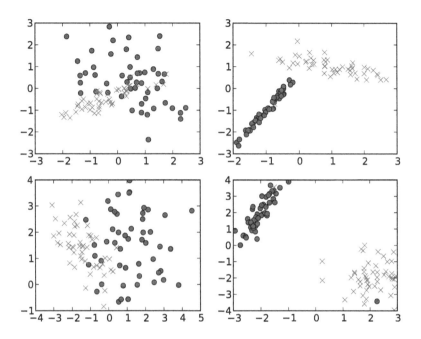

Figure 2.3: Binary classification problems with varying degrees of separability.

what extent data is identically distributed, we use two standard divergence measures: Kullback-Leibler (KL) divergence and Jensen-Shannon divergence. For the single cluster assumption and low-density separation, we introduce within-class and between-class scatter.

Divergence measures say something about the similarity of samples and distributions. They can be used to assess the representativity of samples or the distance between distributions $P(\mathbf{x})$ and $Q(\mathbf{x})$, and we will primarily use them as an estimate of to what extent our data is sampled identically.

KL divergence is often used to test the representativity of samples or to measure the distance between two distributions. KL divergence is defined as:[3]

$$KL(P, Q) = \sum_{\mathbf{x}} P(\mathbf{x}) \log \frac{P(\mathbf{x})}{Q(\mathbf{x})} \tag{2.1}$$

KL divergence is thus asymmetric, and typically $KL(P, Q) \neq KL(Q, P)$.

[3]KL divergence is also known as relative entropy and is the cross-entropy between the two distributions $(-\sum_{\mathbf{x}} P(\mathbf{x}) \log Q(\mathbf{x}))$ minus the entropy of the base distribution $(-\sum_{\mathbf{x}} P(\mathbf{x}) \log P(\mathbf{x}))$.

Jensen-Shannon divergence is the symmetric version of KL divergence:

$$D_{\text{JS}}(P, Q) = \frac{1}{2} D_{\text{KL}}(P, M) + \frac{1}{2} D_{\text{KL}}(Q, M) \tag{2.2}$$

with M the average of P and Q.

Both divergence measures assume we know the two distributions in advance. In practice, we typically have a finite sample of labeled data and some test instances and we cannot compute $P(\mathbf{x})$ and $Q(\mathbf{x})$ in general. If we assume independence (of binary, discrete variables), we can compute KL divergence as follows:[4]

```
def KLDisc(X1,X2):
    P=np.array([(X1[:,i].mean()+.5/X1.shape[0]) for i in range(X1.shape[1])])
    Q=np.array([(X2[:,i].mean()+.5/X2.shape[0]) for i in range(X2.shape[1])])
    div=sum(multiply(P,log(P/Q)))
    return div
```

The shape attribute of numpy arrays is the number of rows and, if any, columns. In this case, we compute a smoothed mean for each column, that is each of our features.

[102] present an algorithm for estimating KL divergence from finite samples using nearest neighbor search using KD trees[5] to do efficient nearest neighbor search when we cannot assume independence of variables.

```
from scipy.spatial import cKDTree as KDTree

def KLDiv(X1,X2):
    n,d=X1.shape
    m,dy=X2.shape
    xtree=KDTree(X1)
    ytree=KDTree(X2)
    r=xtree.query(X1,k=2,eps=.01,p=2)[0][:,1]
    s=ytree.query(X1,k=1,eps=.01,p=2)[0]
    diff=r/s
    return -np.log(diff).sum() * d / n + np.log(m/(n-1))
```

Within-class and between-class scatter rely on the notion of *co-variance*. The average observed value of a variable (its mean) is often referred to as its expected value. ⏹ It is important to note that, if two variables x_1 and x_2 have the same expected value, say 20, it does *not* follow that $P(x_1 = 40) = P(x_2 = 40)$, i.e., that the two variables are equally likely to turn out 40. Say you are looking at a corpus of spam emails; x_1 is an integer-valued variable encoding the occurrences of the word "Keiro," and x_2 encodes the number of occurrences of the word "the." Say also that half of the spam emails in your corpus are written by someone with pseudonym "Keiro" writing his pseudonym 40

---

[4]In this implementation we use Krichevsky-Trofimov smoothing (adding half a count to each variable). See Section 2.3 for more on smoothing.

[5]A KD tree is a binary tree in which every node is a k-dimensional point. See [85] for details on how KD trees are used for nearest neighbor search.

times in his signature. The number of occurrences of "the" ranges from 15–25. Both variables have expected value 20, but $P(x_1 = 40) = .5$, while $P(x_2 = 40) \sim 0$.

The variance of a variable is the expected value of the difference between the expected value of a variable and its actual value squared, i.e., an estimate of how much the variable is likely to deviate from its mean value, μ:

$$\sum_{i=1}^{N} (x_j^i - \mu_j)^2 \tag{2.3}$$

This is also a measure of the observed spread or scatter when we plot the observed values of the variable.

Co-variance is a measure of how dependent two variables are:

$$\text{Cov}(x_j, x_k) = \sum_{i=1}^{N} (x_j^i - \mu_j)^2 (x_k^i - \mu_k)^2 \tag{2.4}$$

The Python in-built function cov takes the transpose of a dataset and computes a *co-variance matrix*:

$$\begin{pmatrix} \text{Cov}(x_1, x_1) & \cdots & \text{Cov}(x_1, x_n) \\ \vdots & \vdots & \vdots \\ \text{Cov}(x_n, x_1) & \cdots & \text{Cov}(x_n, x_n) \end{pmatrix}$$

The **within-class scatter** is computed by weighting the covariances of the class variables by class probabilities:

$$\sum_{y \in \mathcal{Y}} P(y) \sum_{\langle y, \mathbf{x}_i \rangle \in T} (\mathbf{x}_i - \mu_y)(\mathbf{x}_i - \mu_y)^T \tag{2.5}$$

The **between-class scatter** is simply:

$$\sum_{y \in \mathcal{Y}} (\mu_y - \bar{\mathbf{x}}))(\mu_y - \bar{\mathbf{x}}))^T \tag{2.6}$$

If the within-class scatter is small, the cluster assumption is likely to hold. Similarly, if the between-class scatter is large, the low-density separation assumption is likely to hold.

In Python the within-class scatter can be computed as follows:

```python
def Sw(X1,y):
    sw=0
    classes=unique(y)
    for i in range(len(classes)):
        indices=np.squeeze(np.where(y==classes[i]))
        d=np.squeeze(X1[indices,:])
        classcov=np.cov(np.transpose(d))
        sw+=float(np.shape(indices)[0])/X1.shape[1]*classcov
    return sw
```

2.2   NEAREST NEIGHBOR

Nearest neighbor is the conceptually simplest of classifiers, but has nevertheless found many applications in NLP. The main reason for this is that nearest neighbor is a *non-parametric* learning algorithm, i.e., an algorithm that does not make any assumptions about how the data can be modeled, except that if two data points $\mathbf{x}$ and $\mathbf{x}'$ are similar, they tend to belong to similar classes y and y'. Two similar data points are near each other in the feature representation space, and the nearest neighbor classifier, in its simplest form, just says that we should label an unseen data point by the label of its nearest neighbor in the previously seen data, i.e., our labeled data. The only thing left is to introduce a distance metric. Three example distance metrics are Euclidean distance, Manhattan distance, and Hamming distance. Euclidean distance should be familiar to the reader. The Manhattan distance between $\mathbf{x}$ and $\mathbf{x}'$ is $\sum_i |x_i - x_i'|$. Finally, Hamming distance simply counts the features where the two feature vectors differ. This corresponds to counting the dimensions in which two data points have different coordinates.

Consider the toy dataset in Figure 2.1. The Hamming distance of the unlabeled data point is 2 to the first data point, 3 to the second, and 1 to the third. The nearest neighbor is therefore the third of our labeled data points. Consequently, we predict the new email to be non-spam.

The Python implementation of nearest neighbor is now straightforward.

```python
from __future__ import division
from scipy.spatial.distance import euclidean as D
import numpy as np

class NearestNeighbor():
    def __init__(self):
        self.name="Nearest Neighbor"
    def fit(self,X,y):
        self.X_train=X.toarray()
        self.y_train=y
    def score(self,X,y):
        correct=0
        assert X.shape[1]==self.X_train.shape[1]
        for i in range(X.shape[0]):
            ind=np.array([D(X[i,:],self.X_train[j,:])
                  for j in range(self.X_train.shape[0])]).argmin()
            if y[i]==self.y_train[ind]:
                correct+=1
        return (correct/X.shape[0])
```

The code implements the nearest neighbor algorithm as a Python class with a fitting method and a scoring method. This is also the format adopted in SkLearn, which means that we can now import our learning algorithm as any other algorithm in SkLearn. We first convert the sparse matrices to numpy arrays. For each test data point $\langle y_i, \mathbf{x}_i \rangle$, we compute an $N \times 1$ array of distances to $\langle y_i, \mathbf{x}_i \rangle$. The argmin function returns the index of the shortest distance. Finally, we output an accuracy on the test data.

The nearest neighbor classifier is extremely expressive. While the other learning algorithms we will introduce learn linear discriminants, i.e., require the classes to form smooth and complete clusters, the nearest neighbor algorithm can, in principle, learn a chess board distribution of two classes (black and white) or any other geometric distribution. The nearest neighbor classifier divides space in the form of what is known as a Voronoi tessellation.[6]

While nearest neighbor is very expressive, it is also very unstable in the sense that a slightly different sample may introduce a very different decision boundary. This can also be phrased in terms of the bias-variance trade-off [70]: expressive models introduce very little inductive bias, but nearest neighbor performance varies a lot with different samples and across problems. One way to decrease variance or instability is to increase the number of nearest neighbors used to determine the class of unseen data points. This leads us to k-nearest neighbor classification. In a k-nearest neighbor classification, we simply let the k-nearest neighbors of the unseen data point vote on its class. In the code above, we would have to store a list of indices of nearest neighbors rather than just the single-nearest neighbor index we get from argmin. This can be achieved using the numpy function argsort.

[6]A Voronoi tessellation is a division of space by points $p_k \in P$ such that the region containing the point p_k consists of every point whose distance to p_k is less than or equal to its distance to any of the other points in P. The segments are then the points that are equidistant to two or more points in P.

In SkLearn, k-nearest neighbor comes as an in-built function.

```
from sklearn.neighbors import KNeighborsClassifier as knn

clf=knn(n_neighbors=1)
clf.fit(X_train,y_train)
print clf.score(X_test,y_test)
```

If n_neighbors is set to 1, we do nearest neighbor classification, but set to k, we let the k-nearest neighbors vote on each of our unseen data points. Note that now we can estimate probabilities by taking the number of votes k_i on a particular class y_i over k:

$$\hat{p}(y_i|\mathbf{x}) = \frac{k_i}{k} \tag{2.7}$$

Obviously, brute-force nearest neighbor search will be time-expensive on large datasets, since it runs in time linear in the size of the training set, but the SkLearn function implements several algorithms for fast nearest neighbor search. On HOCKEY-BASEBALL, a nearest neighbor classifier achieves an accuracy of 89.8%. Our first implementation is about 50 times slower than the SkLearn implementation. SkLearn actually *does* brute-force search in the above example. The reason that it is so much faster is because it encodes data points as sparse vectors. This is an important observation. Sparse feature vectors are extremely important for large-scale natural language learning problems, which are typically high-dimensional, but where each data point is described by the occurrence of only a small subset of features.

Consider the accuracy of k-nearest neighbor with varying k from the plot in Figure 2.4a. Performance initially goes up with increasing k. The plot illustrates how k-nearest neighbor with small k is prone to over-fitting.

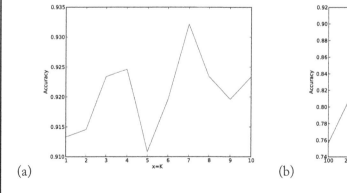

(a)   (b)

Figure 2.4: (a) Performance of k-nearest neighbor with varying k on HOCKEY-BASEBALL. (b) Learning curve for 1-nearest neighbor on HOCKEY-BASEBALL.

☞ [7] Mooney [95] shows that k-nearest neighbor out-of-the-box typically does not perform well with bag-of-words models. Bag-of-words models include thousands of dimensions, but, only a subset of them tend to be predictive. While methods based on early discrimination such as decision trees typically perform worse [95], k-nearest neighbor puts equal weight on all features and the distance between two data points is to a large extent determined by non-predictive features. Of course, this problem can be solved by feature selection or by using k-nearest neighbor with a distance metric that incorporates some form of feature weighting.

For efficiency and memory reasons, k-nearest neighbor does not scale very well either, as already discussed. We, therefore, cannot apply it directly to GWEB-EMAILS-TRANSITIONS with 65,520 data points and 448,949 features. Figure 2.4b represents a learning curve for 1-nearest neighbor on HOCKEY-BASEBALL for small amounts of data. The fact that nearest neighbor methods are prone to overfitting means they suffer from data sparsity. Combined with their lack of scalability, this sometimes prohibits the application of nearest neighbor methods to large-scale NLP tasks. Chapter 3 will introduce dataset condensation techniques that make nearest neighbor methods more efficient.

2.3   NAIVE BAYES

Naive Bayes performs much better than nearest neighbor on HOCKEY-BASEBALL, with an accuracy of 97.5% compared to 89.8%. In fact, nearest neighbor methods with standard distance metrics do not typically perform well with bag-of-words representations. The reason is that all features are equally important in nearest neighbor for the distance between a labeled and an unseen data point. In Naive Bayes, this is not the case.

There is a lot to be said about the Naive Bayes classifier. It is a Bayesian network and a linear classifier (see below), but, for now, we introduce it as a classification algorithm *on a par* with nearest neighbor. The Naive Bayes classifier implements three intuitions: (a) if we have observed non-spam emails more often than spam emails (2/3), for example, we should be more likely to predict that emails are not spam; (b) all features can potentially change our belief about whether an email is spam or not; (c) the features are evidence in favor of spam or not, independently of each other. It is (b) and (c) that distinguish the Naive Bayes classifier from other Bayesian networks.

We will use probabilities to encode beliefs. If you are familiar with basic probability theory,[8] you also know the Chain Rule stating that $P(A, B) = P(A)P(B|A) = P(B)P(A|B)$, e.g., the probability of meeting Noam Chomsky and Francois Hollande down at the corner is the probability of either meeting Noam and meeting Francois, given you just met Noam, or vice versa. If the two events are assumed to be independent of each other, $P(A, B) = P(A)P(B)$. Since, all things being equal, it is more likely to observe a single event than a conditional event (if you condition on a rare

---

[7]The ☞ symbol is used to indicate that the current paragraph includes one ore more important "rules of thumb."

[8]Otherwise, consult [83] (Section 2.1) or John Goldsmith's tutorial at `http://humanities.uchicago.edu/faculty/goldsmith/Industrial/Probability.htm`

event), the independence assumption (c) makes the Naive Bayes less vulnerable to data sparsity than other Bayesian networks.

Now we want to compute $P(y|\mathbf{x})$ for a new data point $\mathbf{x}$ to determine its most likely class y. We can use the Chain Rule to isolate $P(y|\mathbf{x})$:

$$P(y|\mathbf{x}) = \frac{P(y)P(\mathbf{x}|y)}{P(\mathbf{x})} \tag{2.8}$$

Since you rarely observe the same (or anything close to the same) email twice, we cannot estimate $P(\mathbf{x}|y)$ directly, but assumption (c) allows us to replace the equation above, known as Bayes' Rule, with the following:

$$P(y|\mathbf{x}) = \frac{P(y)\prod_i P(x_i|y)}{P(\mathbf{x})} \tag{2.9}$$

To find the most likely class we just need to compute $\hat{y} = \arg\max_{y \in \mathcal{Y}} P(y)\prod_i P(x_i|y)$. This is known as the maximum a posteriori (MAP) estimate. Consider now the toy dataset in Figure 2.1 again. To compute the probability of the unlabeled email being spam we need:

$$
\begin{array}{ll}
P(\text{spam}) & 1/3 \\
P(\text{zebra} = 0 \mid \text{spam}) & 1 \\
P(\text{viagra} = 1 \mid \text{spam}) & 1 \\
P(\text{venus} = 1 \mid \text{spam}) & 0
\end{array}
$$

The product of the probabilities in the right column is obviously 0. It turns out that the same holds for the probability of $P(\text{non-spam}|\langle 0, 1, 1\rangle)$, because none of our non-spam emails includes the word "Viagra." This turns out to be a real problem in high-dimensional problems such as document classification. The trick is to *smooth* probabilities. The simplest smoothing technique, known as Laplace smoothing, is to assume every feature-value pair has been observed at least once. The prior probability of spam, i.e., $P(\text{spam})$, is now 2/5 rather than 1/3, and it now holds that $P(\text{spam})\prod_i P(x_i|\text{spam}) \sim 6\%$ and $P(\text{non-spam})\prod_i P(x_i|\text{non-spam}) \sim 4\%$, and the Naive Bayes classifier with Laplace smoothing therefore predicts that the unlabeled email is spam.

Here is a simple Python implementation of Naive Bayes for binary variables.

```python
class NaiveBayes():
    def __init__(self,alpha=1.0):
        self.name="Naive Bayes"
        self.smoothing=alpha
    def fit(self,X,y):
        y_pos=y>0
        y_neg=y<=0
        self.pos_prior=y.mean()
        self.neg_prior=1-y.mean()
        self.pos_lik={}
        for i in range(X.shape[1]):
            self.pos_lik[i]=(
                X[y_pos,i].sum()+self.smoothing/
                (X[y_pos].sum()+self.smoothing*X.shape[1])
                )
        self.neg_lik={}
        for i in range(X.shape[1]):
            self.neg_lik[i]=(
                X[y_neg,i].sum()+self.smoothing/
                (X[y_neg].sum()+self.smoothing*X.shape[1])
                )
    def score(self,X,y):
        correct=0
        assert X.shape[1]==self.features
        for i in range(X.shape[0]):
            pos_joint=self.pos_prior
            for j in range(X.shape[1]):
                if X[i,j]>0:
                    pos_joint+=np.log(self.pos_lik[j])
            neg_joint=self.neg_prior
            for j in range(X.shape[1]):
                if X[i,j]>0:
                    neg_joint+=np.log(self.neg_lik[j])
            if pos_joint>neg_joint and y[i]>0:
                correct+=1
            elif neg_joint>=pos_joint and y[i]<=0:
                correct+=1
        return correct/X.shape[0]
```

The fit-call basically builds a table of smoothed probabilities, i.e., prior probabilities of class and likelihoods of individual features given class. Given that we only have two classes and all normalized features (either binary or tfidf), we get probabilities by computing mean values in our data. We use α for the smoothing parameter to adhere to SkLearn conventions. The SkLearn implementation of Naive Bayes is called as follows:

```
from sklearn.naive_bayes import BernoulliNB as nb

clf=nb()
clf.fit(X_train,y_train)
print clf.score(X_test,y_test)
```

Unlike nearest neighbor, Naive Bayes learns linear decision boundaries. Linear classifiers can be formulated as weight vectors $\mathbf{w}$ such that the classification decision of the linear classifier on $\mathbf{x}$ becomes $\text{sign}(\mathbf{w} \cdot \mathbf{x} + b) = \text{sign}(\sum_i w_i x_i + b)$, i.e., if the dot product of the model $\mathbf{w}$, which contains a weight for every feature, and the data point vector $\mathbf{x}$ is $> -b$, the model predicts positive class. In this formulation the Naive Bayes classifier is:

$$\mathbf{w} = (\log \theta_1 - \log \theta_0)^\top \tag{2.10}$$

and

$$b = (\log P(y = 1) - \log P(y = 0)) \tag{2.11}$$

where θ_y is the multinomial distribution of a document within the class y. See the next section for more on linear classifiers.

👍 Performance on GWEB-EMAIL-TRANSITIONS is 87.9% and we obtain the learning curve in Figure 2.5. The starting point of Naive Bayes is typically good and optimal performance is often reached earlier than with other methods, indicating that Naive Bayes (with appropriate smoothing) suffers less from data sparsity than classifiers such as k-nearest neighbor. Therefore, Naive Bayes is often a good choice if you only have a small amount of training data.

👍 It has often been noted that Naive Bayes does remarkably well in empirical evaluations in spite of its unrealistic independence assumption [63]. One reason is that Naive Bayes has fewer parameters than related models (more inductive bias) and is therefore less prone to over-fitting. It is also worth noting that dependence is particularly important for estimating probabilities, but in classification, we only care about the rank order of classes [43]. Naive Bayes is notoriously bad at predicting probabilities [96]. If your application requires reliable probability estimates, it is better to use logistic regression.

2.4   PERCEPTRON

The perceptron and Naive Bayes are both linear classifiers, but the learning algorithms are very different. While Naive Bayes computes $\mathbf{w}$ once and for all, the perceptron learning algorithm [110] updates the weights in $\mathbf{w}$ at a fixed rate in multiple passes over the data.

A perceptron c consists of a weight vector $\mathbf{w}$ with a weight for each feature, a bias term b, and a learning rate α. For a data point $\mathbf{x}_j$, $c(\mathbf{x}_j) = 1$ iff $\mathbf{w} \cdot \mathbf{x} + b > 0$, else 0. In other words, a data point $\mathbf{x}_j$ is classified as positive if the dot product of the model and $\mathbf{x}_j$ is $> -b$. The threshold for classifying something as positive is thus $-b$. The dot product is the sum of products, here in Python code:

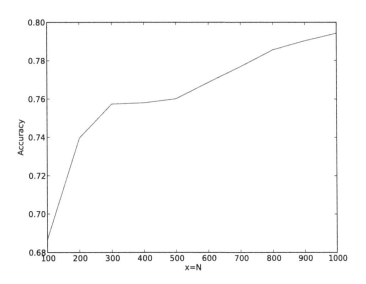

Figure 2.5: Learning curve for Naive Bayes on Gweb-Email-Transitions.

```
def dotprod(w,x):
    return sum([w[i]*x[i] for i in range(len(w))])
```

The bias term is typically left out by adding an extra variable to our data with fixed value -1. The perceptron learning algorithm now works by maintaining $\mathbf{w}$ in several passes over the data (see Figure 5.2). Say the algorithm at time i is presented with a labeled data point $\langle \mathbf{x}_j, y_j \rangle$. The current weight vector $\mathbf{w}^i$ is used to calculate $\mathbf{x}_j \cdot \mathbf{w}^i$. If the prediction is wrong, an update occurs:

$$\mathbf{w}^{i+1} \leftarrow \mathbf{w}^i + \alpha(y_j - \text{sign}(\mathbf{w}^i \cdot \mathbf{x}_j))\mathbf{w} \tag{2.12}$$

The numbers of passes K the learning algorithm does (if it does not arrive at a perfect separator any earlier) is typically fixed by a hyper-parameter. Unless explicitly stated, the number of passes is fixed to 5 in our experiments below.

Consider a single-pass run on the toy dataset in Figure 2.1. We initialize the model as $w = \langle 0, 0, 0, 0 \rangle$, where the 4th weight is the bias term which is encoded as a node always receiving the signal -1. Say $\alpha = 0.1$. The prediction for the first data point is that it belongs to the negative class, since $0 \cdot 0 + 1 \cdot 0 + 0 \cdot 0 + -1 \cdot 0 = 0$. This is wrong, so we update the weights, leading to:

$$w = \langle 0 + 0.1(1 - 0)0, 0 + 0.1(1 - 0)1, 0 + 0.1(1 - 0)0, 0 + 0.1(1 - 0) - 1 \rangle = \langle 0, 0.1, 0, -0.1 \rangle$$

The next two data points are correctly classified as negative data points, so no additional updates are made in the first pass over the data.

Python code implementing perceptron learning is presented in Figure 2.7. In addition to the dot product code above, it also uses a function for sign.

```
def sign(x):
    return 1 if x>0 else 0
```

The SkLearn implementation of perceptron is in a module called `linear_models`, also including logistic regression and stochastic gradient descent.

```
from sklearn.linear_models import Perceptron as perc

clf=perc()
clf.fit(X_train,y_train)
print clf.score(X_test,y_test)
```

Performance is 97.5% on Hockey-Baseball and 90.8% on Gweb-Email-Transitions. The learning curve on Gweb-Email-Transitions is presented in Figure 2.6. Mooney [95] shows that perceptron does relatively well with bag-of-words models. Later in this chapter we introduce extensions of both Naive Bayes and perceptron to structure prediction problems.

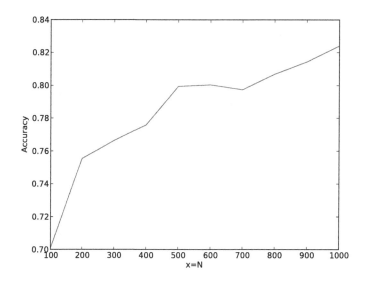

Figure 2.6: Learning curve for perceptron on Gweb-Email-Transitions.

The perceptron learning algorithm is computationally efficient and conceptually simple, and therefore very popular, but, it also has a number of weaknesses. The algorithm does not prefer scoring functions with larger margins and it is very unstable in the sense that the final scoring function depends heavily on the data sample. The instability of the perceptron learning algorithm means it is very prone to overfitting data, much like the nearest neighbor classifier.

2.4.1   LARGE-MARGIN METHODS

Several improvements to the perceptron algorithm have been proposed in the last decade, including the averaged perceptron [30, 50], the voted perceptron [50], the margin perceptron, which updates weights to keep a fixed margin to examples, passive-aggressive learning [35], confidence-weighted classification [44, 90], and AROW [34]. While these linear classification methods differ in how well they optimize the margin, the large margin decreases the probability of error when data is generated i.i.d. at random (under the Smoothness Assumption).

Related algorithms include the well-known and widely used logistic regression and support vector machines (SVMs) [32, 137]. Here, we briefly describe averaged perceptron [50] and passive-aggressive perceptron [33].

Averaged Perceptron

The perceptron learning algorithm is prone to overfitting, but one way overfitting can be reduced is by averaging the weight vectors w^1, w^2, ... There are two options, either to store all weight vectors (one for each update) and average them after learning, or, to average after every single update (early update). While hard to analyze theoretically, averaged perceptron learning performs well and tends to classify data with large margins [50]. Averaging is an indirect form of regularization. Regularization can also be performed directly by adding a term to the perceptron loss function that minimizes the weights in a way similar to support vector machines. The code in Figure 2.7 also does averaged perceptron learning by setting a parameter. There is also a parameter for setting a particular form of averaged perceptron learning where more weight is put on recent updates; this is a component in the forgetron model [39], but only a small part of it. 👍 It often leads to better results in averaged perceptron learning to put more weight on recent updates.

Passive-aggressive

The passive-aggressive algorithm [33] is presented in Figure 2.8. The algorithm only differs from averaged perceptron in line 5. Both averaged perceptron and the passive-aggressive algorithm are passive learning algorithms that do not update their weight vectors on instances that are classified correctly with the current model. However, while averaged perceptron updates its weights vector by a fixed rate, the passive-aggressive is also *aggressive* in the sense that it forces $\mathbf{w}^{i+1}$ to classify the latest instance correctly, regardless of the step-size required.

2.5   COMPARISONS OF CLASSIFICATION ALGORITHMS

Figure 2.9 and Figure 2.10 present an evaluation of the three main learning algorithms—nearest neighbor, Naive Bayes, and perceptron—over 25 randomly selected cross-domain datasets in 20

```python
class Perceptron(object):
    def __init__(self,alpha=1.0,n_iter=5,RandomInit=True,Averaged=True,Forgetron=True):
        self.alpha=alpha
        self.randominit=RandomInit
        self.averaged,self.forgetron=Averaged,Forgetron
        self.iters=n_iter
        self.updates=0
    def fit(self,X,y):
        if self.randominit:
            self.model=[random.random() for i in range(X.shape[1]+1)] # +1 for bias
        else:
            self.model=[0 for i in range(X.shape[1]+1)] # +1 for bias
        if self.averaged:
            self.arrmodel=np.array(self.model)
        for i in range(self.iters):
            for n in range(X.shape[0]):
                d=[y[n]]+[X[n,j] for j in range(X.shape[1])]+[-1]
                dp=dotprod(self.model,d[1:])
                pred=sign(dp)
                if pred!=d[0]:
                    self.update(d,pred)
                if self.averaged:
                    if self.forgetron:
                        self.arrmodel+=(np.array(self.model)*self.updates)
                    else:
                        self.arrmodel+=np.array(self.model)
        if self.averaged:
            if self.forgetron:
                self.model=[self.arrmodel[i]/((self.updates**2-self.updates)/2)
                                    for i in range(self.arrmodel.shape[0])]
            else:
                self.model=[self.arrmodel[i]/self.updates
                                    for i in range(self.arrmodel.shape[0])]
    def update(self,yx,y_hat):
        y,x=yx[0],yx[1:]
        self.model=[self.model[i]+self.alpha*(y-y_hat)*x[i]
                            for i in range(len(self.model))]
        self.updates+=1
    def score(self,X,y):
        corr=0
        for n in range(X.shape[0]):
            d=[y[n]]+[X[n,i] for i in range(X.shape[1])]+[-1]
            dp=dotprod(self.model,d[1:])
            pred=sign(dp)
            if pred==d[0]:
                corr+=1
        return corr/X.shape[0]
```

Figure 2.7: Python code for perceptron learning.

1: dataset $X = \{\langle y_i, \mathbf{x}_i \rangle\}_{i=1}^{N}$
2: $\mathbf{w}^0 = 0, \mathbf{v} = 0, i = 0$
3: **for** $k \in K$ **do**
4:      **for** $n \in N$ **do**
5:          $\mathbf{w}^{i+1} \leftarrow \arg\min_{\mathbf{w} \in \mathbb{R}^n} \|\mathbf{w}^{i+1} - \mathbf{w}^i\|$ s.t. $\text{sign}(\mathbf{w}^{i+1} \cdot \mathbf{x}_n) = y_n$
6:          $\mathbf{v} \leftarrow \mathbf{v} + \mathbf{w}^{i+1}$
7:          $i \leftarrow i + 1$
8:      **end for**
9: **end for**
10: **return** $\mathbf{w} = \mathbf{v}/(N \times K)$

Figure 2.8: Passive-aggressive learning.

Newsgroups. Figure 2.10 gives you the individual results, where you can see that nearest neighbor is almost consistently worse across the board (see the discussion on page 19). The right column results in Figure 2.9 are correlation coefficients comparing performance on a cross-domain dataset with estimated KL divergence between source and target. We see that the correlations are all negative, which makes intuitive sense. The bigger the domain difference, the worse the performance.

learner	acc	$\rho(KL)$
nb	0.753	−0.22
perc	0.709	−0.09
nn	0.614	−0.27

Figure 2.9: Empirical comparison of nearest neighbor, Naive Bayes and perceptron on 25 randomly selected cross-domain datasets in 20 Newsgroups, performance correlated with KL divergence.

👍 From the results, it also seems that perceptron is less sensitive to KL divergence than nearest neighbor and Naive Bayes (though results are not statistically significant). It is not surprising that nearest neighbor is very sensitive to KL divergence, since we know that inductive bias reduces the chance of over-fitting data. There is a second possible explanation for the observed effect: some of the most frequent predictive words are likely to transfer. In the sports domains, we talk about "leagues" and "points," for example. In computer science, we talk about "systems" and "performance." Computing nearest neighbors, we put equal weight on all our features, whereas perceptrons assign more weight to frequent, predictive features.

Finally, we also tried to correlate performance with within-class scatter. The results are presented in Figure 2.11. We see that within-class scatter is negatively correlated with the performance of Naive Bayes, but uncorrelated with the performance of the nearest neighbor classifier. This is expected, since the Naive Bayes classifier learns a linear decision boundary. Quite surprisingly,

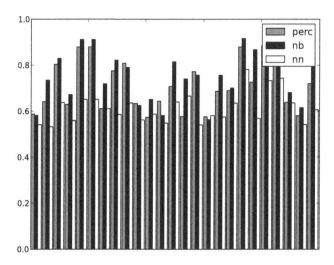

Figure 2.10: Empirical comparison of nearest neighbor, Naive Bayes and perceptron on 25 randomly selected cross-domain datasets in 20 Newsgroups.

within-class scatter is also uncorrelated with the performance of the perceptron, indicating that the perceptron is more sensitive to other data characteristics. Note also that, on this subset of data, the perceptron is better than Naive Bayes. In Figure 2.9, it was the other way around. We return to the issue of predicting performance across biased datasets in Chapter 6.

learner	acc	$\rho(wcs)$
nb	0.842	−0.34
perc	0.868	−0.03
nn	0.627	−0.01

Figure 2.11: Empirical comparison of nearest neighbor, Naive Bayes, and perceptron on 25 randomly selected cross-domain datasets in 20 Newsgroups, performance correlated with within-class scatter.

There are a few large-scale comparisons of supervised learning algorithms in the literature, including [21]. I also recommend having a look at this website:

http://mlcomp.org

2.6   LEARNING FROM WEIGHTED DATA

Later, it will become useful to be able to assign weights to data points. Learning from weighted data is used in boosting [3, 51] and in our implementation of Expectation-Maximization [97], but, we will make extensive use of algorithms learning from weighted data when correcting bias in available labeled data in Chapter 4. Some data points may be more relevant than others in the target distribution and we will use importance weights to adapt our labeled data to the target distribution. Can we, in some way, modify our algorithms so that they learn from weighted data and learn less from data points with low weights and more from data points with high weights?

2.6.1   WEIGHTED k-NEAREST NEIGHBOR

In k-nearest neighbor, it is easy to learn from weighted data. Simply let the k-nearest neighbors vote on the class of the previously unseen instance and weight the vote of each neighbor by that data point's weight. Weighted k-nearest neighbor is currently not supported by SkLearn, but, it is easy to modify the k-nearest neighbor version of the from-scratch code in Section 2.2 to implement weighted voting.

2.6.2   WEIGHTED NAIVE BAYES

Weighted Naive Bayes *is* supported in SkLearn and works by weighting the MAP estimates.[9] For illustration, consider the toy dataset from Figure 2.1, reprinted here with weights in the left column:

β	y	zebra	viagra	venus
$\beta_1 : 0.6$	spam	0	1	0
$\beta_2 : 0.2$	non-spam	1	0	0
$\beta_3 : 0.3$	non-spam	1	0	1
	?	0	1	1

In the unweighted case, the prior probability of observing spam was $1/3$. In the weighted case, $P(\text{spam}) = 0.6/1.1$. $P(\text{zebra} = 0 \mid \text{spam})$ is still 1, but while $P(\text{zebra} = 0 \mid \text{non-spam})$ was $1/2$, it is now $3/5$.

2.6.3   WEIGHTED PERCEPTRON

In weighted perceptron [22], which is also supported in SkLearn, we make the learning rate depend on the current instance, using the following update rule on $\mathbf{x}_n$:

$$\mathbf{w}^{i+1} \leftarrow \mathbf{w}^i + \beta_n \alpha (y_n - \text{sign}(\mathbf{w}^i \cdot \mathbf{x}_n))\mathbf{x}_n \tag{2.13}$$

The intuition is that we are willing to update our weights more if we misclassify important data points than when we are misclassifying less important data points.

---

[9]In SkLearn, weighted Naive Bayes is obtained by passing an array of data point weights using the `sample_weight` option when fitting to data.

2.6.4   WEIGHTED LARGE-MARGIN LEARNING

The passive-aggressive algorithm can also be weighted. Say we update our weight vector by a step-size α in the passive-aggressive algorithm in order to classify a data point $\langle y_n, \mathbf{x}_n \rangle$ correctly. We instead update by a stepsize $\beta_n \alpha$, where β_n is the instance weight assigned to $\langle y_n, \mathbf{x}_n \rangle$. [123] also present an instance-weighted version of the MIRA algorithm [35] and apply it to dependency parsing. [67] present an instance-weighted learning algorithm for support vector machines. The weighted SVM objective, presented in [67], is supported by SkLearn providing a wrapper for the LibSVM 3.1 implementation.[10]

2.7   CLUSTERING ALGORITHMS

Clustering is learning without labels. How can you learn from unlabeled data? Obviously, you cannot learn a function from $\mathcal{X}$ to $\mathcal{Y}$, but, we can try to group the elements in $\mathcal{X}$ into natural classes. In a lot of the applications we are interested in, we do not have directly applicable labeled data, but, we still have an interest in dividing data up in manageable subgroups.

Consider, for example, Internet search. You formulate a search query and the search engine returns several thousands of websites. Maybe your search query was ambiguous or underspecified, and it turns out you are only interested in a small subset of the returned websites. Since we do not know anything about the irrelevant websites in advance, we do not know what the labeled data that would enable us to discriminate between relevant and irrelevant websites would look like. However, if we could group the documents into a small number of clusters, we could display one or two prototypical hits from each cluster and have the user pick the cluster of interest.

In NLP, we are typically interested in clustering words or documents, but, there are also applications of clustering dependency trees [106] or paragraphs [105], for example. Unsupervised learning algorithms are also used for novelty detection and dimensionality reduction. Below, we introduce some of the most widely used unsupervised learning algorithms (clustering algorithms) and relate them to the supervised algorithms introduced above.

2.7.1   HIERARCHICAL CLUSTERING

Consider the dataset in Figure 2.12. How many clusters do you see in the data? Two or three? The colored centers indicate that there are three clusters, and the dataset was actually generated from three isotopic Gaussian blobs. However, not knowing that, we might as well assume two groups.

For many problems in NLP, we do not really know the number of classes. There are POS tagsets for English, for example, with 10, 31, 45, or more tags. There is no consensus on the right number of syntactic categories for English. The same holds in topic modeling or word sense induction, for example.

Hierarchical clustering methods build hierarchies of clusters. A cluster hierarchy has a top node, which is the cluster that includes all previously seen data points. The leaf nodes in the hierarchy

---

[10]http://www.csie.ntu.edu.tw/~cjlin/libsvm/

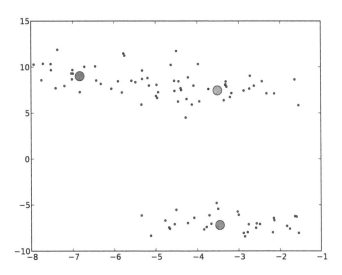

Figure 2.12: Randomly generated clusters.

correspond to single data points. You can now cut the hierarchy at any depth, or in some other way, to give you clusters of varying granularity. ⏹ Note that hierarchical clustering does not necessarily give you decision functions that enable you to assign new data points to existing clusters. A standard hierarchical clustering algorithm is presented in Figure 2.13.

1: Dataset $X = \{\mathbf{x}_i\}_{i=1}^N$, a distance function d
2: $C = \{\{\mathbf{x}_i\} \mid \mathbf{x}_i \in X\}$ # each data point a cluster
3: **while** $\{\mathbf{x}_i\}_{i=1}^N \notin C$ **do**
4: $\quad c_j, c_k \leftarrow \arg\min_{c_{j'}, c_{k'} \in C, j' \neq k'} d(c_{j'}, c_{k'})$
5: $\quad C \leftarrow C \cup \{(c_j \cup c_k)\}$
6: **end while**
7: **return** C

Figure 2.13: Hierarchical clustering.

The simplest hierarchical clustering algorithm is probably single-link hierarchical clustering. The notion of *single linkage* refers to how we compute the distance between two clusters c_j, c_k. Say

d refers to Manhattan distance and is defined for pairs of data points. We can then extend d to pairs of clusters by:

$$d(c_j, c_k) = \min_{\mathbf{x} \in c_j, \mathbf{x}' \in c_k} d(\mathbf{x}, \mathbf{x}') \qquad (2.14)$$

If we take the distance between the data points farthest away from each other to be the distance between two clusters (replacing minimization with maximization in Equation 2.14), we get *all-links* hierarchical clustering. Finally, we can take the average distance between pairs of data points in the two clusters (average-link hierarchical clustering).

single linkage $\quad d(c_j, c_k) = \min_{\mathbf{x} \in c_j, \mathbf{x}' \in c_k} d(\mathbf{x}, \mathbf{x}')$

all linkage $\quad d(c_j, c_k) = \max_{\mathbf{x} \in c_j, \mathbf{x}' \in c_k} d(\mathbf{x}, \mathbf{x}')$

average linkage $\quad d(c_j, c_k) = \frac{\sum_{\mathbf{x} \in c_j, \mathbf{x}' \in c_k} d(\mathbf{x}, \mathbf{x}')}{|C|}$

Figure 2.14: Distance between clusters in hierarchical clustering.

Let us apply the single-link hierarchical clustering algorithm to our toy spam dataset, for illustration. We have the data points $\langle 0, 1, 0 \rangle$, $\langle 1, 0, 0 \rangle$, $\langle 1, 0, 1 \rangle$, $\langle 0, 1, 1 \rangle$. We have two pairs of data points with distance 1, so we build the following hierarchical structure:

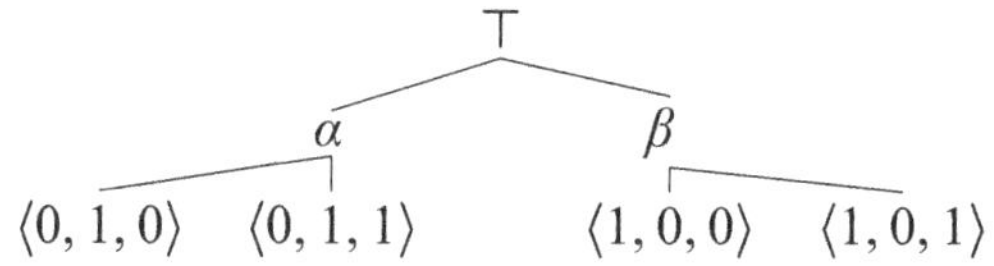

Note that the binary clustering we would get from cutting the tree at the second level groups the test data point correspond to spam emails in our labeled data (for exactly the same reason the nearest neighbor rule classifies it as spam).

Ward's method is very similar to average-link hierarchical clustering. It formalizes the notion of merging cost:

$$\Delta(c_j, c_k) = \sum_{i \in c_j \cup c_k} d(\mathbf{x}_i - m_{c_j \cup c_k})^2 - \sum_{i \in c_j} d(\mathbf{x}_i - m_{c_j})^2 - \sum_{i \in c_k} d(\mathbf{x}_i - m_{c_k})^2 \qquad (2.15)$$

It then replaces $d(c_{j'}, c_{k'})$ in line 6 in hierarchical clustering (Figure 2.13) with the left-hand side of Equation 2.15. The algorithm is greedy and constrained by previous choices, and the sum-of-squares for a given number k of clusters is usually larger than the minimum, and even larger than what k-means (below) will achieve. Ward's algorithm can be used to initialize k-means, however, leading k-means into better local maxima. In SkLearn, clustering algorithms do not come with `predict` methods, but, here is an example of a clustering experiment.

```
from sklearn.cluster import Ward
clu=Ward(n_clusters=2)
clu.fit(X_train)
print sklearn.metrics.v_measure_score(y_train,clu.labels_)
```

We return to evaluation metrics for clustering, incl. V-measure used here, in Section 2.7.4.

2.7.2 k-MEANS

The k-means algorithm selects k centers for a given dataset. The cost of the solution is the squared distance from each data point to its nearest center, and the task is to minimize this cost. This cost is the first component of the merging cost in Ward's method (Equation 2.15), i.e., the cost of the final k clusters. The cost minimization in k-means problem is NP-hard, but heuristic algorithms such as Lloyd's algorithm are known to work well in practice. We present Lloyd's algorithm in Figure 2.15.

1: $E = \{e_1, \ldots, e_k\} \leftarrow$ **random.choice**$(\{\mathbf{x}\}_{i=1}^N, k)$
2: $C_j = \{m_j\}$ for $j \leq k$
3: **for** $r \in R$ **do**
4:     **for** $n \in N$ **do**
5:         $C_j \leftarrow C_j \cup \{\mathbf{x}_n\}$ s.t. $\arg\min_{j \leq k} d(e_j, \mathbf{x}_n)$
6:     **end for**
7:     $\{m_j\} \leftarrow$ **centroid**(C_j) for $j \leq k$
8: **end for**

Figure 2.15: k-means (Lloyd's algorithm). **Note:** We use R for passes, rather than K, to avoid confusion.

In line 1 we randomly select k data points $E = \{e_1, \ldots, e_k\}$, which we will assume are the centroids of our clusters. The algorithm then proceeds in R passes over the data by alternating between assigning all data points to their nearest centroid to build the actual clusters (line 5) and (re-)computing the actual centroids of these clusters (line 7).

The algorithm, being heuristic, is not guaranteed to converge in the global optimum and it is common to run it multiple time with random restarts. The assignment step in line 5 is also sometimes referred to as the expectation step (E-step), and the update step in line 7 is sometimes referred to as the maximization step (M-step), establishing an analogy with Expectation Maximization (EM). It turns out that Lloyd's k-means is an instance of generalized EM (see next subsection).

In SkLearn:

```
from sklearn.cluster import KMeans
clu=KMeans(k=2)
clu.fit(X_train)
sklearn.metrics.v_measure_score(y_train,clu.labels_)
```

2.7.3   EXPECTATION MAXIMIZATION

Expectation maximization (EM) is often introduced in terms of Gaussian mixture models, but, in this book, EM will refer more broadly to a wrapper method applicable to any weighted learning algorithm that can produce a confidence score for its predictions. EM will be introduced this way in Chapter 3, but here, we will limit ourselves to the standard case of Gaussian mixture models.

Gaussian mixture models assume data was generated by a mixture of Gaussian distributions parameterized by their mean μ (expected value) and variance σ^2:

$$P(x) = \frac{1}{\sqrt{2\pi}\sigma} e^{\frac{-(x-\mu)^2}{2\sigma^2}} \tag{2.16}$$

Say we had a one-dimensional dataset, and two normal distributions with parameters $\mu_1 = .5, \sigma_1^2 = .5$ and $\mu_2 = 1, \sigma_2^2 = .5$. The two distributions have the same variance, but different means. For any new instance, e.g., $x = .6$, we can now compute the probability of that instance in the two distributions and predict the class that makes the instance most probable. This will be the class that most densely populates the region around the new instance. What happens if data is multi-dimensional? If the variables in our dataset are independent, we can compute the probability of $\mathbf{x}$ as the product of the probability of the individual features. Such a model is called a Gaussian mixture model.

EM for Gaussian mixture models as a clustering algorithm works by randomly setting $\mu_1, \mu_2, \sigma_1^2, \sigma_2^2$ (often we set σ_i^2 to the variance in the entire dataset) and a mixing parameter $\hat{\pi}$ (encoding the prior probability of data being generated by one of the Gaussians). In the E-step we compute $P(y_j \mid \mathbf{x}, \theta)$ with $j \in \{1, 2\}$. This can be computed by application of Bayes' rule. We then reestimate $\mu_1, \mu_2, \sigma_1^2, \sigma_2^2$ from this distribution, apply the model to data, etc. k-means is the special case of hard EM, where $\sigma_1^2 = \sigma_2^2$ and the covariance matrix is the identity matrix. Intuitively, this means that regions are circular rather than ellipsoid.

2.7.4   EVALUATING CLUSTERING ALGORITHMS

In classification, we can evaluate our models by their accuracy, precision, or recall on held-out data, but, how do we evaluate clustering algorithms? In the NLP community two methods are often used: F-measure and V-measure.

F-measure is simply the optimal F-score under different assignments of clusters to classes in the held-out data. Recall that F-score is the harmonic mean of precision and recall. V-measure is defined as the harmonic mean of homogeneity and completeness. Homogeneity measures to what extent all members of a cluster are in the same class in the held-out data. It is defined as follows:

$$1 - \frac{-\sum_{k \in K} \sum_{c \in C} \frac{|c \cup k|}{N} \log \frac{|c \cup k|}{|k|}}{-\sum_{c \in C} \frac{|c|}{N} \log \frac{|c|}{N}} \tag{2.17}$$

Completeness, on the other hand, measures to what extent all members of a class in the held-out data are clustered together. Clustering algorithms are, of course, best evaluated in terms of downstream applications, but this is beyond the scope of this book. The application of clustering algorithms in clusters-as-features (Section 3.2) can be seen as a related way of evaluating clustering algorithms.

2.8 PART-OF-SPEECH TAGGING

Structure prediction is the prediction of a set of interrelated variables. Structure prediction arises when we break the independence assumption in supervised learning, i.e., the first part of the i.i.d. assumption (Section 2.1); if the output variables become interdependent, we need to predict them jointly. This chapter presents the intuitions behind a few simple, yet popular, approaches to structure prediction, namely, hidden Markov models [7], the structured perceptron for POS tagging [30], transition-based dependency parsing [143], and the extension of the structured perceptron to edge-factored dependency models [89]. The two first can be considered sequential analogues of Naive Bayes and perceptron. See [118] for a book-length introduction to structure prediction. In POS tagging and dependency parsing, we make the simplifying assumption that sentence-level analyses are independent of each other (which in some cases they are not).

The canonical approach to POS tagging is using *hidden Markov models* (HMMs) [23, 27]. The difference between Naive Bayes and (simple) HMMs is best illustrated by formulating them as Bayesian networks.

A Bayesian network is a graph $G = \langle E, V \rangle$ of edges E connecting vertices V corresponding to observable and unobservable variables. Graphs here will be understood as directed acyclic graphs, deliberately excluding undirected graphical models, which are beyond the scope of this book. An edge between two variables x_i and x_j then can be said to encode domain knowledge that x_i causes x_j. In addition to the graph structure, a Bayesian network also specifies a conditional probability distribution at each node. In the case of discrete variables only, the distributions give us the probability of the values of the current variable, given all combinations of the previous variables' values.

In a Bayesian network, the probability of a particular set of values is the product of the probability of each value given the parent nodes' values:

$$P(x_1, \ldots, x_m) = \prod_{i \geq 1}^{m} P(x_i \mid \{x_j \mid \langle j, i \rangle \in E\}) \tag{2.18}$$

Recall that in Naive Bayes:

$$P(y, x_1, \ldots, x_m) = P(y) \prod_{i \geq 1}^{m} P(x_i \mid y) \tag{2.19}$$

It follows that, in order to present this as a Bayesian network, the vertex corresponding to the class label y should have no incoming edges, while all other vertices (corresponding to our observable variables) should only have an incoming edge going from the y-labeled vertex. See Figure 2.16 for a graphical presentation of Naive Bayes with five observable variables. The generative story that

Naive Bayes implements is easily "read off" the graph: first, we decide on the class of an object, and then, we draw values of all observable variables independently of each other, only conditioned on the object's class.[11]

HMMs are used for sequence labeling, but, let us first motivate modeling POS tagging as a sequence labeling problem rather than as mere classification. Classification methods rely on the assumption that data is independently drawn, but this assumption is violated in POS tagging. To see this consider the famous example:

(1) Time flies like an arrow.

Both the readings N-V-ADV-DET-N and N-N-V-DET-N are available, but the reading N-N-ADV-DET-N does not seem available—independently of context. If we decide *flies* is a noun, *like* has to be a verb. If we decide *flies* is a verb, *like* has to be an adverb. Classification algorithms are not designed to handle such dependencies, but, there is an obvious hack that may come in handy. If we classify the words in (1) one at a time, left to right, we can condition our decision on our previous decision by making our previous decision observed for the next classification problem. This hack is sometimes referred to as *consecutive classification*. This potentially leads to an accumulation of errors, since our decisions will often be conditioned on previous mistakes, but there is a more serious problem with this approach. Consider the example:

(2) The British left waffles on Falklands

This sentence also has a least two interpretations, depending on whether *left* is a noun or a verb, but the most likely reading is probably that waffles were left by the British on Falklands. Consecutive classification would, however, be likely to produce the other reading. In the context of a determiner, *British* is likely to be an adjective. In the context of an adjective, *left* is likely to be a noun, and then *waffles* is likely to be a verb.

The change in the most likely reading of (2), as we read more words, is often referred to as a *garden path effect* in psycholinguistics. The structure prediction models will give us means of modeling garden path effects.

The right structure in Figure 2.16 represents an HMM with five observable variables and five hidden output variables. The generative story is, again, easily read off: you generate a hidden variable, say a part of speech, then you generate its observable variance and the next hidden variable, and so on. This network can be used to assign syntactic categories to a sentence with five words (our output variables) with limited modeling of garden-path effects. Consider an HMM for four word sentences. Say we only have four parts of speech (ADJ, DET, NOUN, VERB) and have learned some parameters giving us the probability distributions:

---

[11]Generative stories and models are important in statistical machine translation [18] and unsupervised dependency parsing [76]; the two cited articles may also be a good place to start if you are not familiar with the concept of generative stories, or how it is used in NLP.

given/	ADJ	DET	NOUN	VERB
ADJ	0.2	0.0	0.7	0.1
DET	0.5	0.0	0.5	0.0
NOUN	0.0	0.1	0.3	0.6
VERB	0.0	0.4	0.2	0.4

given/	The	British	left	waffles
ADJ	0.0	0.4	0.6	0.0
DET	0.1	0.0	0.0	0.0
NOUN	0.0	0.2	0.2	0.6
VERB	0.0	0.0	0.7	0.3

Below we compute the most probable sequence(s) of values for the output variables, given the observable variables *The British left waffles* using Equation 2.18. The candidate readings discussed above are equally likely in this model, but, note how the preferred reading changes as we see more words. After two words *British* is predicted to be an adjective, after three words a noun.

0.0:ADJ	0.2:DET-ADJ	0.024:DET-ADJ-ADJ	0.0:DET-NOUN-VERB-ADJ
0.1:DET	0.0:DET-DET	0.0:DET-ADJ-DET	0.0:DET-NOUN-VERB-DET
0.0:NOUN	0.1:DET-NOUN	0.028:DET-ADJ-NOUN	0.00504:DET-NOUN-VERB-NOUN
0.0:VERB	0.0:DET-VERB	0.042:DET-NOUN-VERB	0.00504:DET-ADJ-NOUN-VERB
The	British	left	waffles

Figure 2.16: Naive Bayes and hidden Markov models as Bayesian networks.

We note that decoding with HMMs only requires storing $m \times n$ probabilities where m is the number of hidden output variables and n is the number of observable ones. The chart-based algorithm leading to tables such as the one above is often referred to as the Viterbi algorithm, outputting a Viterbi path or sequence. It is relatively easy to implement Viterbi decoding using two SkLearn classifiers—one for emission probabilities and one for transition probabilities.

Today, HMMs are often replaced by conditional random fields [79] or structured perceptrons [30]. The structured perceptron is similar to the averaged perceptron, except training data points are sequences rather than single objects. Consequently, the structured perceptron does not predict a class label but a sequence of labels (using Viterbi decoding, as in the above example). However, we update only the features at the positions where the predicted labels are different from the true labels. We do this by adding weight to features present in the correct solution and subtracting weight to features present in the predicted solution. In order to train the structured perceptron, we use Viterbi decoding to compute the predicted sequence for the current training point and update our weights accordingly. A publicly available and easy-to-modify Python reimplementation of the structured perceptron can be found here:

<code>https://github.com/gracaninja/lxmls-toolkit</code>

2.9 DEPENDENCY PARSING

In the previous section, we saw that it is suboptimal to model POS tagging as a classification problem; the same holds for dependency parsing. If we train a binary classifier to predict whether two words w, w' form a head-dependency pair, we can run through all candidate heads for any word. If we want to label the dependencies, we can subsequently run through all predicted arcs and use a multinomial classifier to predict the most likely label, given what we know about the head word and its dependent. However, reducing dependency parsing to classification this way does not model the intricate dependencies between grammatical functions. For example, there is no guarantee that a classification-based model does not predict all words to be subjects of the main verb, which would be linguistically impossible. Or, for another example, take the sentence:

(3) John saw the man on the mountain with a telescope.

If the first prepositional phrase attaches to the main verb *saw*, the second prepositional phrase cannot attach to the object *man*. If the first prepositional phrase attaches to the object, this is perfectly possible.

In this section, we consider two approaches to the structure prediction problem of dependency parsing. In one approach, our models will be parameterized over the transitions of a transition system (different, but not too different from a finite state automaton); in the other, our models will be parameterized over sub-structures of dependency trees or just over candidate dependencies. The first approach is called *transition-based* dependency parsing, the second approach *graph-based* dependency parsing. We refer the reader to Kübler et al. [78] for a more thorough discussion.[12]

Formally, a dependency tree for a sentence $x = w_1, \ldots, w_n$ is a tree $T = \langle V = \{0, 1, \ldots, n\}, A \rangle$ with $A \subseteq V \times V$ the set of dependency arcs. Each vertex corresponds to a word in the sentence, except 0 which is the root vertex, i.e., for any $i \leq n$ $\langle i, 0 \rangle \notin A$. A dependency tree is acyclic. A tree is projective if every vertex has a continuous projection, i.e., if and only if for every arc $\langle i, j \rangle \in A$ and node $k \in V$, if $i < k < j$ or $j < k < i$ then there is a subset of arcs $\{\langle i, i_1 \rangle, \langle i_1, i_2 \rangle, \ldots, \langle i_{k-1}, i_k \rangle\} \in A$ such that $i_k = k$.

2.9.1 TRANSITION-BASED DEPENDENCY PARSING

Finite state automata consists of states and transitions defined on states and input symbols. An automaton accepts strings if there is a sequence of valid transactions from an initial state to a final state, reading the input symbols. In transition-based dependency parsing, analogously, we convert

---

[12]We will try to use a notation similar to the one used in Kübler et al. [78] to make it easier to supply what is said here with their more detailed account.

our input symbols to configurations (our representations of states) and, learn transitions between them. If we can reach a final state, we accept the sentence—and, as an important side-product, we have obtained a dependency structure for the sentence.

Unlike with finite state automata, we will assume a "guide" that tells us where to go in any given state. This guide will be a classifier learned from data estimating a function from feature representations of configurations to transitions. Our configurations not only represent input symbols, but also, some of the previous decisions we made. A configuration $c = \langle \sigma, \beta, A \rangle$ consists of a stack of words σ, a buffer of words β, and a set of dependency arcs A, i.e., triples of a head word, a dependency label, and a dependent word.

It is customary to assume an artificial root node w_0 (see Figure 1.2) so that all (actual) words are assigned a head in a dependency analysis. The initial configuration is then $\langle [w_0]_\sigma, [w_1, \ldots, w_n]_\beta, \emptyset \rangle$. A final state is any configuration of the form $\langle \sigma, []_\beta, A \rangle$, i.e., any state in which the buffer is empty.

In the arc standard scheme [100] there are three possible transitions. The SHIFT transition takes a word from the buffer β and moves it to the top of the stack σ. The LEFT-ARC transition removes the top word w_i from the stack and adds a dependency from w_i to the first word on the buffer to A. The RIGHT-ARC transition removes the first word w_j on the buffer and takes the top word w_i on the stack, places w_i back on the buffer, and adds a dependency from w_i to w_j to A. In each derivation step, the parser is guided to apply one of these transitions to the current configuration. See Figure 2.17 for an example derivation.

SHIFT	...	John smokes Lebanese	
LEFT-ARC	..., John	smokes Lebanese	
SHIFT	...	smokes Lebanese	John ← smokes
RIGHT-ARC	..., smokes	Lebanese	
SHIFT	...	... smokes	smokes → Lebanese
LEFT-ARC	...	...	ROOT → smokes

Figure 2.17: Example derivation in transition-based dependency parsing.

Since the guiding classifier has access to its previous decisions when predicting the next transition, the transition-based parsing algorithm described above is actually using consecutive classification to do structure prediction. The most widely used transition-based algorithms can only derive *projective* dependency trees, i.e., trees without crossing branches, but recently, several non-projective transition-based parsing algorithms have been proposed [29, 98].

2.9.2   GRAPH-BASED DEPENDENCY PARSING

The basic idea in graph-based dependency parsing is that the score (or probability) of a dependency tree $G = \langle V, E \rangle$ factors through the scores of subtrees, and, in edge-factored models, the factors are the edges E. In standard notation:

$$\text{score}(G) = \sum_{(w_i, r, w_j) \in A} \lambda_{(w_i, r, w_j)} \tag{2.20}$$

where λ is our model parameters. This just means that the score of a dependency tree is the sum of the score of its edges. Since most dependency parsers typically use a linear model $\mathbf{w}$ (learned by a structured perceptron, for example), $\lambda_{(w_i, r, w_j)}$ is typically a place holder for $\mathbf{x} \cdot \mathbf{w}$, where $\mathbf{x}$ is the feature representation of the edge (w_i, r, w_j).

Just like with HMMs, we now have two challenges: We need (a) a way of finding the best dependency tree given a model (decoding), and (b) a way to learn a good model from data (learning). If we limit ourselves to projective dependency trees, we can use decoding algorithms from constituent-based parsing, but, if we allow crossing branches, these algorithms are not applicable. Fortunately, as long as we assume that our scoring function factors through the scores of edges, we can use so-called minimum spanning tree algorithms for decoding. We refer the interested reader to McDonald et al. [89], as well as to Kübler et al. [78].

In order to learn edge-factored models using a linear classifier, we need to establish a mapping from a candidate edge (w_i, r, w_j) to a feature representation. Relevant features could be the word forms and parts of speech of the dependent and head tokens, but also morphological information, information about neighboring words, and the direction and length of the candidate dependency. The linear model $\mathbf{w}$ can then be learned using structured perceptron, for example, and used to score all candidate edges, producing an $n \times n$-matrix of scores for an input sentence of n words. The minimum spanning tree algorithm can then be used to extract the optimal dependency tree from the matrix.

See [88] for an empirical comparison of transition-based and graph-based dependency parsing. The quick and dirty summary is that, while transition-based parsers allow us to condition our choices on derivation history, conditioning on past decisions also means that errors accumulate. One consequence is that transition-based parsers typically perform worse on dependencies close to the root node, since these dependencies are the last to be added to the dependency structure. For the same reason, graph-based parsers are usually better at predicting long dependencies and at predicting the syntactic heads of verbs and conjunctions.

CHAPTER 3

Semi-Supervised Learning

The intuition behind semi-supervised learning is that we can exploit the marginal distribution of unlabeled data, typically available in larger volumes than labeled data, to learn better models than with labeled data alone. I tell my son that $\mathbf{x}_i$ is a cow and $\mathbf{x}_j$ is a horse, but then he starts to label other four-legged animals he sees in the countryside, gradually refining his decision boundary.[1] However, semi-supervised learning also often leads to degradation in performance. Sometimes degradation is due to invalid assumptions. Many semi-supervised methods, such as transductive support vector machines [73] and most graph-based semi-supervised learning algorithms, assume that decision boundaries run through sparse regions. These algorithms obviously perform poorly on data generated by two heavily overlapping Gaussians, for example. See Figure 3.1 for a problem where the optimal decision boundary lies in a dense region.

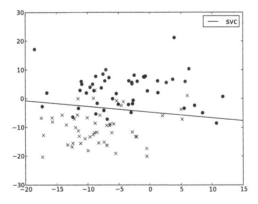

Figure 3.1: Decision boundary in dense region (svc='support vector classification').

This chapter introduces some semi-supervised learning methods that have been used in the NLP literature. We distinguish between wrapper methods to turn any or most supervised learning algorithms into semi-supervised ones (self-training, co-training, and EM, for example), methods that augment labeled data with clusters learned from unlabeled data, and methods specific to nearest neighbor algorithms. See also [1] for an introduction to semi-supervised learning for NLP covering several topics not included here, including semi-supervised support vector machines, as well as [148]

[1]For a nice study of human use of unlabeled data and the effect it has on our decision boundaries, see [149].

for an emphasis on graph-based, semi-supervised algorithms and an introduction to semi-supervised SVMs. When possible, we use a notation similar to theirs to bridge between the three books. Other approaches to semi-supervised learning not covered here include [5, 117, 134].

Semi-supervised learning can also be used for learning under bias by exploiting the marginal distribution of unlabeled data sampled from the target domain for which you have no labeled data. Such algorithms may be very effective and are widely used in NLP for domain adaptation, but, they only work if the expected error of the base classifier trained on the labeled source data is reasonably low on the unlabeled target data. Chapter 4 discusses the application of semi-supervised learning algorithms to learning under bias in more detail and presents algorithms that may correct bias in cases where expected error on target data is high.

3.1   WRAPPER METHODS

The wrapper methods we will discuss here are related in the following ways, and we will begin our review of these methods bottom-up:

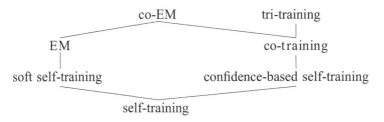

You can think of this graph as representing subsumption relationships between the code needed to implement these methods. Self-training does not take a lot of code once you have your base learner (see Figure 3.4). Add a line of code to the code for self-training, and you have soft self-training. You add one or two lines to that, and you have EM. Same goes for co-training, which you can combine to implement co-EM, and so on. Now for the methods.

3.1.1   SELF-TRAINING

Self-training is probably the simplest possible approach to semi-supervised learning. We have a classifier c learned from a set of labeled data points $L = \{\langle y_i, \mathbf{x}_i \rangle\}_{i=1}^{N}$, but, we also want to exploit information in a large volume of unlabeled data $U = \{\mathbf{x}_i\}_{i=1}^{M}$, typically with $M > N$. Why don't we just use c to label the data in U so that we can learn from it? The self-training algorithm, which in its simplest form does exactly that, is presented in Figure 3.2. The general idea is very simple, but leaves us with a large number of choices.

Obviously, our initial classifier will mislabel some of the data in U. If we now proceed to learn from the concatenation of the original labeled data and the newly labeled data, including a lot of mislabeled data, our performance on held-out data will often decrease. Since we are learning from noisier data, this is not surprising. To accommodate this, it is customary to introduce a `select` function (line 4) that selects only a subset of the newly labeled data, which we then concatenate with L. A common strategy here is to import only data points that are labeled confidently by the classifier, say with a confidence of $> 90\%$. Note, however, that this may skew our training data. If we had only a small amount of labeled data and large volumes of unlabeled data, and our consecutive classifier in transition-based dependency parsing (see Chapter 2) was only confident when predicting RIGHT-ARC, we could easily end up predicting only right-branching structures.

Another choice to make is whether to delete previously imported data in each round of self-training, i.e., if we replace the first occurrence of L in line 4 with L_0 and L in line 1 and 2 with L_0. Self-training with deletion is sometimes called *delible* self-training [1].

1: $L = \{\langle y_i, \mathbf{x}_i \rangle\}_{i=1}^N, U = \{\mathbf{x}_i\}_{i=1}^M$
2: $c \leftarrow \texttt{train}(L)$
3: **while** stopping criterion is not met **do**
4:     $L \leftarrow L + \texttt{select}(\texttt{label}(U, c))$
5:     $c \leftarrow \texttt{train}(L)$
6: **end while**
7: **return** c

Figure 3.2: Self-training.

Finally, we need to settle on a stopping criterion (line 3). Held-out data, or cross-validation, is typically used to estimate a reasonable number k of fixed rounds, but in some cases a good selection criterion, combined with techniques for making self-training more robust, allows you to go on until convergence. Techniques to make self-training more robust include throttling, balancing, and pooling [1]. Throttling means that we only select k data points in each pass over the unlabeled data, while balancing simply refers to using a `select` function that selects only the k most confidently labeled data points in each class. Pooling refers to always using a (randomly sampled) subset of the unlabeled data; combined with a confidence-based selection criterion this is different from throttling. See Chapter 5 for general techniques for making learning algorithms more robust when available labeled data is biased.

Figure 3.3 presents a successful application of self-training (plot 0). Here we pool a single data point at a time and always label it, even if our confidence is low. The three other methods plotted are discussed below. 👍 Pooling only a single data point in each pass over the unlabeled data often leads to improved performance. While pooling only a single data point in each pass over the unlabeled data may be very time-consuming, this often leads to significantly better results than the simple self-training algorithm. If your base learner accepts weighted input, combining this kind of conservative pooling with soft labeling of unlabeled data (see below) is often a good choice in practice.

Self-training is widely used in NLP, but many negative results have also been reported [1, 28, 109, 126, 127, 128]. In POS tagging, Huang et al. [68] use self-training to obtain improvements over

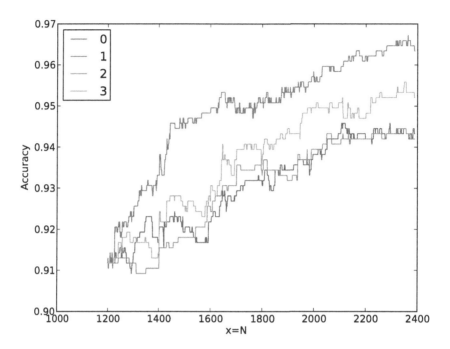

Figure 3.3: Comparison of (0) self-training, (1) soft self-training, (2) random co-training, and (3) regular co-training on HOCKEY-MOTORCYCLES to BASEBALL-AUTOS (pool size=1).

a simple bigram POS tagger. Subramanya et al. [129] report improvements over a supervised baseline using self-trained conditional random fields for POS tagging, but also introduce a superior semi-supervised learning algorithm. In parsing, McClosky et al. [86] showed how self-training a parser on reranked output can lead to significantly better results than state-of-the-art supervised parsers. Huang et al. [69] showed how an ensemble of self-trained parsers trained on disjoint data labeled by the ensemble can lead to improvements over both supervised and semi-supervised baselines.

👍 The last two papers indicate that self-training is more effective in two-stage systems where the second stage informs the first after changing or improving the output of the first stage.

Several authors have proposed to refine self-training by selecting unlabeled data that the supervised parser is likely to assign correct structures. Reichart and Rappoport [109], for example, suggest that the number of unknown words is a good indicator of the usefulness of a target sentence in self-training. Rehbein [108] proposes to use a trigram language model over POS sequences to select unlabeled data for dependency parsing.

Finally, consider our implementation of self-training using SkLearn conventions in Figure 3.4. We load the labeled data and two copies of the unlabeled data into the same matrix. Loading two copies of the unlabeled data will be useful for implementing soft self-training later. We assume U_size is an integer giving us the number of unlabeled data points, and we derive L_size, the number of labeled data points. Because it will be useful later on, we will think of the self-training procedure as alternating between an E-step (line 4 in Figure 3.4) and an M-step (line 5). In the M-step we simply retrain our classifier and in the E-step we label unlabeled data. The code presented here comes with two parameters, the number of passes made over the unlabeled data and the pool size considered. The learner is set to perceptron and does five passes over the unlabeled data by default.

```
class Selftraining():
    def __init__(self,learner=perc(),iters=5,pool=100):
        self.learner=learner
        self.iters=iters
        self.poolsize=pool

    def fit(self,X_train,y_train,U_size):
        L_size=X_train.shape[0]-U_size*2
        weights=[1]*L_size+[0]*U_size*2
        def M_step():
            self.learner.fit(X_train,y_train,sample_weight=weights)
        def E_step():
            for i in np.random.randint(L_size,
                                       X_train.shape[0]-U_size,
                                       size=self.poolsize):
                if float(self.learner.predict(X_train[i,:]))==1:
                    weights[i]=1
                else:
                    weights[i+U_size]=1
        M_step()
        for _ in range(self.iters):
            E_step()
            M_step()

    def score(self,X,y):
        return self.learner.score(X,y)
```

Figure 3.4: Python code for self-training.

3.1.2 CO-TRAINING

Co-training, introduced by Blum and Mitchell [14], is another attempt to make self-training more robust. There is something counterintuitive about self-training. How can one learn from oneself? The answer of course is that we are learning from data, not from ourselves, but the many negative results with self-training reported in the literature (see above) suggest that in self-training we are often led astray by our mispredictions on unlabeled data. This is probably why self-training is more effective in two-stage systems. Co-training offers an alternative and intuitively appealing solution to this dilemma by introducing a second perspective on data.

Co-training usually relies on a feature split giving us two *views* on data. The algorithm presented in Figure 3.5. Blum and Mitchell [14] proved that, if the two views are sufficient, redundant, and conditionally independent, co-training can be successful. Abney [2] proved that weak dependence can also guarantee successful co-training. Blacan et al. [6] weakened the necessary assumptions even further. Recently single-view variants have been introduced [56, 80] and Wang and Zhou [139] showed that co-training can work with sufficiently diverse classifiers trained on the same view. See below for more on single-view co-training. In our two-view co-training experiments, we use a random feature split. This is common practice and often works in spite of the lack of theoretical guarantees.

Figure 3.3, for example, illustrates a successful application of co-training. As already mentioned, we pool a single unlabeled data point at a time and label it. The *random* co-training algorithm randomly selects one of the views in order to label each unlabeled data point, whereas regular co-training let both classifiers label the unlabeled data points simultaneously.

1: $L = \{\langle y_i, \mathbf{x}_i \rangle\}_{i=1}^{N}, U = \{\mathbf{x}_i\}_{i=1}^{M}$
2: $c \leftarrow \texttt{train}(L)$
3: **while** stopping criterion is not met **do**
4: $\quad c_1 \leftarrow \texttt{train}(\texttt{view}_1(L))$
5: $\quad c_2 \leftarrow \texttt{train}(\texttt{view}_2(L))$
6: $\quad L \leftarrow L + \texttt{select}(\texttt{label}(U, c_1)) + \texttt{select}(\texttt{label}(U, c_2))$
7: **end while**
8: $c \leftarrow \texttt{train}(L)$
9: **return** c

Figure 3.5: Co-training.

Co-training was applied to POS tagging in Clark et al. [28], but has also been applied to word sense disambiguation [91] and sentiment analysis [26].

Single-view co-training refers to the observation that lines 4–5 in Figure 3.5 can easily be replaced by two other lines leading to two different models. For example, we could use two different learners or two different samples of our labeled data. Single-view co-training was first applied to transition-based dependency parsing by Sagae and Tsujii [114], who made their two parsers, c_1 and c_2, diverse by using two different learning algorithms (support vector machines and logistic regression), but also by modifying the training data. Motivated by the observation that the performance of transition-based dependency parsing is often very sensitive to left-to-right order, they trained the logistic regression model on mirrored dependency structures that were afterwards mirrored back to reflect left-to-right order.

3.1.3   TRI-TRAINING

Tri-training [80] takes things a step further. Tri-training (Figure 3.6) is a conceptually simple extension of single-view co-training involving three learners that inform each other: let L denote the labeled data and U the unlabeled data. Assume that three classifiers c_1, c_2, c_3 have been trained on L. In [80], the three classifiers are obtained by applying the same learning algorithm to three bootstrap samples of the labeled data. An unlabeled data point in U is labeled for a classifier, say c_1, if the other two classifiers agree on its label, i.e., c_2 and c_3. Two classifiers inform the third. If the two classifiers agree on a labeling, we assume there is a good chance that they are right. In the original algorithm, learning stops when the classifiers no longer change; in generalized tri-training, a fixed stopping criterion estimated on development data is used. The three classifiers are combined by majority voting.

   If the three classifiers are identical, co- and tri-training degenerates to *self-training*. As already mentioned, Li and Zhou [80] obtain diversity training classifiers on bootstrap samples. In their experiments, they consider various learning algorithms, including Naive Bayes. The algorithm is presented in Figure 3.6 in a generalized form where different learners are assumed. Here we return only a single learner, but a common alternative is to return a product of experts.

1: $L = \{\langle y_i, \mathbf{x}_i \rangle\}_{i=1}^{N}, U = \{\mathbf{x}_i\}_{i=1}^{M}$
2: **for** $i \in \{1..3\}$ **do**
3:      $c_i \leftarrow \text{train}_i(L)$
4: **end for**
5: **while** stopping criterion is not met **do**
6:      **for** $i \in \{1..3\}$ **do**
7:          $L_i \leftarrow \emptyset$
8:          **for** $\mathbf{x} \in U$ **do**
9:              **if** $c_j(x) = c_k(\mathbf{x})(j, k \neq i)$ **then**
10:                 $L_i \leftarrow L_i \cup \{\langle c_j(\mathbf{x}), \mathbf{x} \rangle\}$
11:             **end if**
12:         **end for**
13:         $c_i \leftarrow \text{train}_i(L \cup L_i)$
14:     **end for**
15: **end while**
16: **return** c_1

Figure 3.6:   Generalized tri-training.

   Tri-training has been successfully applied to both POS tagging [120] and dependency parsing [126]. Tri-training is easy to implement in SkLearn and we present a comparison over 25 randomly extracted instances of 20 Newsgroups of (i) a supervised perceptron doing 5 passes over the data, (ii) a self-trained perceptron that, after 5 passes over the labeled data, labels all unlabeled data in one pass over the unlabeled data and retrains, and (iii) a tritrained ensemble of three perceptrons initially doing 3, 5, and 7 passes over the data, respectively. The results are presented in the Figure 3.7. Note that tri-training is generally much more robust than self-training. We also note that tritraining improves significantly over a supervised baseline if we use less unlabeled data, e.g., a pool of 20% randomly selected data points. See Figure 3.8 for results. In both experiments we only used the 500 features that correlated best with class according to a χ^2 test.

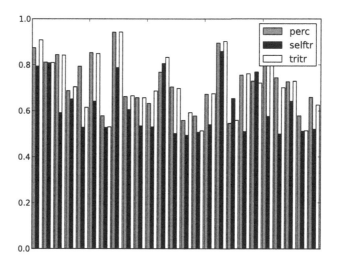

Figure 3.7: Comparison of supervised perceptron, self-training, and tritraining.

3.1.4   SOFT SELF-TRAINING, EM AND CO-EM

In self-training, we assign labels to unlabeled data points and add them to our labeled data. Obviously, we are more confident in some of these labelings than others. Instead of adding only confidently labeled data we can also assign weights to the newly labeled data reflecting our confidence in the labeling.

Say we add two copies of each newly labeled data point $\mathbf{x}$, one for positive class and one for negative class. We then weight the positively labeled data point by the estimated probability $\hat{P}(1|\mathbf{x})$ and the negatively labeled data point $\hat{P}(0|\mathbf{x})$. With our weighted learners we can now learn from the concatenation of the unweighted labeled data and the weighted pseudo-labeled data. In Figure 3.3 we compare the performance of self-training and this other semi-supervised learning

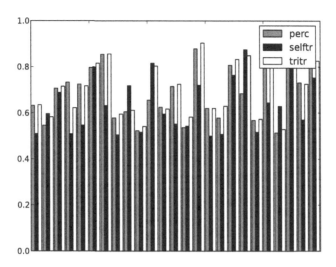

Figure 3.8: Comparison of supervised perceptron, self-training, and *pooled* tritraining.

algorithm, which we will refer to as *soft* self-training. Our base learner in the experiments plotted was (weighted) Naive Bayes.

Instead of pooling batches of unlabeled data in each round of self-training, we can also run over *all* unlabeled data in each round and gradually refine the weights we assign to their negative and positive labels. Call this *delible* soft self-training. Delible soft self-training has been introduced in the literature under another name, namely as a generalization of Expectation-Maximization [1, 41, 97]. On HOCKEY-MOTORCYCLES to BASEBALL-AUTOS, delible soft self-training takes us from 91.17% to 97.10%, where it converges. See Figure 3.9.

The Python code for delible soft self-training is presented in Figure 3.10.

3.2   CLUSTERS-AS-FEATURES

The semi-supervised learning algorithms discussed so far have been wrapper methods applicable to any supervised learning algorithm. Clusters-as-features is also a general technique applicable to any supervised learning algorithm. The technique is simple.

Let L denote the labeled data and U the unlabeled data. Use some clustering algorithm to learn a clustering model m_U from U or $L \cup U$ and augment every data point $\mathbf{x}_n$ in L with a variable that takes the value $m_U(\mathbf{x}_n)$. This new variable encodes the marginal distribution of our unlabeled data and may enable us to better generalize beyond our labeled sample. Note that clusters-as-features is essentially stacked learning (Section 5.2) with a clustering algorithm as level 0 learner.

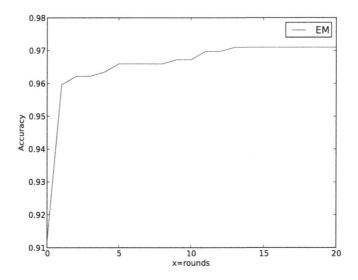

Figure 3.9: Delible soft self-training (EM) on Hockey-Motorcycles to Baseball-Autos.

Clusters-as-features has been successfully applied to both POS tagging [75, 122] and dependency parsing [77, 112]. Turian et al. [135] apply the same technique to NER and NP chunking.

3.3   SEMI-SUPERVISED NEAREST NEIGHBOR

The semi-supervised learning algorithms discussed so far could be applied to any supervised learning algorithm. The next section considers semi-supervised learning algorithms that are tied to a particular supervised algorithm, namely nearest neighbor, either by using nearest neighbor search or because they are motivated explicitly by concerns about the nearest neighbor algorithm, namely label propagation [147], semi-supervised nearest neighbor editing [58], and semi-supervised condensed nearest neighbor [122].

3.3.1   LABEL PROPAGATION

Label propagation [147] is one of the earliest algorithms in the class of graph-based semi-supervised algorithms (see [148] for references). We consider the version using a k-nearest neighbor kernel. This version is similar to self-training with k-nearest neighbor with weighted voting, but with important technical differences. The first step is to construct a k-nearest neighbor graph. In this graph, edges

```
class EM():
    def __init__(self,learner=nb(),iters=5):
        self.learner=learner
        self.iters=iters

    def fit(self,X_train,y_train,U_size): # X_train:train+unl+unl
        L_size=X_train.shape[0]-U_size*2
        weights=[1]*L_size+[0]*U_size*2
        def M_step():
            self.learner.fit(X_train,y_train,sample_weight=weights)
        def E_step():
            for i in np.random.randint(L_size,X_train.shape[0]-U_size,size=U_size):
                if float(self.learner.predict(X_train[i,:]))==1:
                    weights[i]=
                        int(max(self.learner.predict_proba(X_train[i,:]).flatten()))
                    weights[i+U_size]=
                        int(min(self.learner.predict_proba(X_train[i,:]).flatten()))
                else:
                    weights[i]=
                        int(min(self.learner.predict_proba(X_train[i,:]).flatten()))
                    weights[i+U_size]=
                        int(max(self.learner.predict_proba(X_train[i,:]).flatten()))
        M_step()
        for _ in range(self.iters):
            E_step()
            M_step()

    def score(self,X,y):
        return self.learner.score(X,y)
```

Figure 3.10: Code for delible soft self-training (EM).

are weighted such that two nodes that are close to each other are connected by an edge with a large weight:

$$w_{ij} = \exp\left(\frac{-E(\mathbf{x}_i, \mathbf{x}_j)^2}{\sigma^2}\right) \tag{3.1}$$

where E is Euclidean distance, and σ is heuristically set. The algorithm first propagates node labels to neighboring nodes by weighted votes. Each node then collects votes on which class it belongs to, including its own, if labeled. The algorithm works in several iterations (or until convergence) and hard-codes the class of each node after each iteration. Label propagation is implemented in the SkLearn module `semi_supervised` and is easily combined with editing and condensation techniques.

3.3.2   SEMI-SUPERVISED NEAREST NEIGHBOR EDITING

Nearest neighbor methods are said to be lazy methods because no model is learned from the labeled data points. The labeled data points *are* the model. Consequently, as also mentioned in Chapter 2, classification time is proportional to the number of labeled data points. This is, of course, impractical. Many algorithms have been proposed to make nearest neighbor learning more efficient. The intuition behind these algorithms is that only a subset of data points are really important for the decision boundary. In the linearly separable case, SVMs assume only the support vectors are important. In many cases several data points can be disregarded without affecting classification performance. Therefore, the proposed algorithms try to extract a subset of the overall training set that correctly classifies all the discarded data points through the nearest neighbor rule. Intuitively, the algorithms look for good representatives of clusters in the data or discard the data points that are far from the decision boundaries. Such algorithms are called editing, or condensation, algorithms and can be used in combination with intelligent nearest neighbor search or tree-based approximate search [37] to speed up classification.

Finding a subset of the labeled data points may lead to faster and more accurate classification, but finding the best subset is an intractable problem [140]. The need for editing or condensation is particularly important in semi-supervised learning where we rely on a mixture of labeled and unlabeled data points. While the number of labeled data points is typically limited, millions of unlabeled data points may be available. However, it turns out that unlabeled data can also improve editing or condensation, and ultimately, classification performance [58, 122]. This subsection introduces an algorithm referred to as nearest neighbor editing and a semi-supervised extension; the next introduces condensation with a semi-supervised extension.

Nearest neighbor editing is a simple outlier detection technique sometimes used to make nearest neighbor methods more efficient. The algorithm is presented in Figure 3.11. The tuple $c = (k, L)$ is simply the k-nearest neighbor rule applied to the dataset L. The algorithm simply discards all data points whose class can be predicted by their k-nearest neighbors. Nearest neighbor editing is obviously not intended to improve performance, but to improve speed. On cross-domain problems in 20 Newsgroups, 9-nearest neighbor editing typically reduces the dataset by about 90%, but accuracy also drops considerably, in some cases. In other cases, however, performance improves. You typically see more dramatic accuracy drops when data is biased, since outliers are often important to classify instances from new domains.

Guan et al. [58] showed that nearest neighbor editing can take advantage of unlabeled data, labeled by a variant of tri-training where only unlabeled data points that three different classifiers agree on are added to the labeled data. They do two rounds of tri-training to obtain a pseudo-labeled portion of the unlabeled data.

3.3.3   SEMI-SUPERVISED CONDENSED NEAREST NEIGHBOR

The condensed nearest neighbor (CNN) algorithm was first introduced in Hart [64]. CNN can be seen as a simple technique for approximating such a subset of labeled data points. The CNN

Dataset $L = \{\langle y_i, \mathbf{x}_i \rangle\}_{i=1}^N, c_{k,L}$
for $n \in N$ **do**
  if $c_{k,L}(\mathbf{x}_n) = y_n$ **then**
    $L = L \setminus \{\langle y_n, \mathbf{x}_n \rangle\}$
  end if
end for
return $c_{k,L}$

Figure 3.11: Nearest neighbor editing.

Dataset $L = \{\langle y_i, \mathbf{x}_i \rangle\}_{i=1}^N, L' = \emptyset, c_{k,L'}$
for $n \in N$ **do**
  if $c_{k,L'}(\mathbf{x}_n) \neq y_n$ **then**
    $L' = L' \cup \{\langle \mathbf{x}_n, y_n \rangle\}$
  end if
end for
return $c_{k,L'}$

Figure 3.12: Condensed nearest neighbor.

algorithm is defined in Figure 3.12 with T being the set of labeled data points and $T(t)$ the label predicted for t by a nearest neighbor classifier "trained" on T.

Essentially, we discard all labeled data points whose label we can already predict with the current subset of labeled data points. Note that we have simplified the CNN algorithm a bit compared to Hart [64], as suggested, for example, in Alpaydin [4], iterating only once over data rather than waiting for convergence. This will give us a smaller set of labeled data points, and, therefore, classification requires less space and time. Note that while the nearest neighbor classifier cannot be improved by techniques such as bagging [17], CNN can [4].

We also introduce a weakened version of the algorithm which not only includes misclassified data points in the classifier $c_{k,L'}$, but also correctly classified data points which were labeled with relatively low confidence. So $c_{k,L'}$ includes all data points that were misclassified and those whose correct label was predicted with low confidence. $c_{k,L'}$ inspects k-nearest neighbors when labeling new data points, where k is estimated by cross-validation. CNN was first generalized to k-nearest neighbor in Gates [53].

Two related condensation techniques, namely removing typical elements and removing elements by class prediction strength, were argued not to be useful for most problems in NLP in Daelemans et al. [36], but [122] show that CNN often performs about as well as NN, and that a semi-supervised extension of CNN, introduced below, sometimes leads to substantial improvements over k-nearest neighbor methods. The condensation techniques are also very different: while removing typical elements and removing elements by class prediction strength are methods for removing data points close to decision boundaries, CNN ideally only removes elements close to decision boundaries when the classifier has no use of them.

Intuitively, with relatively simple problems obeying the single cluster assumption and the smoothness assumption, e.g., k Gaussians that are unlikely to overlap, CNN and WCNN try to find the best possible representatives for each cluster in the distribution of data, i.e., finding the points closest to the center of each cluster. Ideally, CNN returns one point for each cluster, namely the center of each cluster. However, a sample of labeled data may not include data points that are near the center of a cluster. Consequently, CNN sometimes needs several points to stabilize the representation of a cluster.

When a large number of unlabeled data points that are labeled according to nearest neighbors populates the clusters, chances increase that we find data points near the centers of our clusters. Of course, the centers of our clusters may move, but, the positive results obtained experimentally below suggest that it is more likely that labeling unlabeled data by nearest neighbors will enable us to do better training set condensation.

This is exactly what semi-supervised condensed nearest neighbor (SCNN) is about. We first run a weakened CNN C and obtain a condensed set of labeled data points. To this set of labeled data points we add a large number of unlabeled data points labeled by a k-nearest neighbor classifier T on the original dataset. We use a simple selection criterion and include all data points that are labeled with confidence greater than 90%. We then obtain a new weakened CNN c from the new dataset, which is a mixture of labeled and unlabeled data points. See Figure 3.13 for details.

Semi-supervised condensed nearest neighbor was used for POS tagging in [122].

1: $L = \{\langle \mathbf{x}_i\, y_i \rangle\}_i^N$, $L' = \emptyset$, $L'' = \emptyset$
2: $U = \{\langle \mathbf{x}'_i \rangle\}_i^M$ # unlabeled data
3: **for** $\langle \mathbf{x}_n, y_n \rangle \in L$ **do**
4:     **if** $c_{k,L'}(\mathbf{x}_n) \neq y_n$ or $P_{c_{k,L'}}(\langle \mathbf{x}_n, y_n \rangle | \mathbf{x}_n) < 0.55$ **then**
5:         $L' = L' \cup \{\langle \mathbf{x}_n, y_n \rangle\}$
6:     **end if**
7: **end for**
8: **for** $\langle \mathbf{x}'_i \rangle \in U$ **do**
9:     **if** $P_{c_{k,L'}}(\langle \mathbf{x}'_m, c_{k,L'}(\mathbf{x}'_m) \rangle) > 0.90$ **then**
10:         $L' = L' \cup \{\langle \mathbf{x}'_m, c_{k,L'}(\mathbf{x}'_m) \rangle\}$
11:     **end if**
12: **end for**
13: **for** $\langle \mathbf{x}_n, y_n \rangle \in L'$ **do**
14:     **if** $c_{k,L''}(\mathbf{x}_n) \neq y_n$ **then**
15:         $L'' = L'' \cup \{\langle \mathbf{x}_n, y_n \rangle\}$
16:     **end if**
17: **end for**
18: **return** $c_{k,L''}$

Figure 3.13: Semi-supervised condensed nearest neighbor.

CHAPTER 4

Learning under Bias

Learning under bias refers to learning scenarios where the assumption that data is identically distributed (Section 2.1) does not hold. Data is biased. In the literature, it is common to talk about different kinds of data bias. Data may be slightly differently distributed because of a *sampling bias*. Say we want to build a language model, but, for various reasons, we only have a corpus of sentences of less than 40 words. Our sample is biased, overrepresenting short sentences, containing less connectives or complementizers, for example. It may also be that the distribution has changed (known as population drift [62])—or that the data is sampled from a slightly different distribution. Parsing dialects using annotated standard language may be an example of learning under *distribution bias*. Finally, the data may also be biased because it is annotated with a slightly different problem in mind (known as concept drift). In parsing, this arises if we try to parse across annotation guidelines, or, if we use syntactically annotated corpora to develop semantic parsers.

The distinctions between sampling bias, distribution bias, and problem bias are subtle, however. Is domain adaptation a result of sampling bias, distribution bias, or a problem bias? When we think of domain adaptation as a sampling bias problem, we are typically interested in a domain-independent model of language and we can think of domains as skewed or unrepresentative samples of the language we are modeling. We may also think domain adaptation is about correcting distribution bias and that we are interested in modeling the target domain, which may or may not reflect the same functional relation as the source domain. Often, we would expect the differences across distributions to affect parameter settings, but not the choice of learning algorithm. If domain adaptation is considered a problem bias, we say that parsing newspaper articles and parsing scientific literature are two different problems with different underlying functional relations. Pushing things a bit, we are saying that, in some sense, newspaper articles and scientific literature are written in different languages (with distinct grammars).

👍 A perhaps more useful way of thinking about data biases is as follows. In prediction we are interested in modeling $P(y|\mathbf{x})$. The source data may reflect a different conditional distribution $P(y|\mathbf{x})$ than the target data, which would mean that the bias is not just a sampling bias. Alternatively, the bias may be a difference in the marginal distribution $P(\mathbf{x})$. This assumption is often referred to as the *covariate shift* assumption [116]. Finally, the data bias may be a bias in $P(y)$, often referred to as *class imbalance* [71]. The vague notions of sampling bias, distribution bias, and problem bias can be related to our three-way typology in this way:

	$P(\mathbf{x})$	$P(y)$	$P(y|\mathbf{x})$
sampling bias	MAYBE	MAYBE	NO
distribution bias	MAYBE	MAYBE	MAYBE
problem bias	MAYBE	MAYBE	YES

While sampling bias and problem bias seem contradictory, the notion of distribution bias seems to cover both cases. In NLP domain adaptation, for example, we often talk about distribution bias without assuming a bias in $P(y|\mathbf{x})$, while in other cases we do. Generally, most studies of learning under bias in NLP assume a bias in $P(\mathbf{x})$, but, in word sense disambiguation, the class imbalance problem has attracted some attention, too [150].

In Chapter 3, we considered a range of semi-supervised learning algorithms. Some of these algorithms can be used to correct bias in some cases, but, in this chapter, we will go considerably beyond semi-supervised algorithms in our attempts to adapt to target data. You may wonder how that is possible. How can we adapt to target data beyond learning from a mixture of labeled source data and unlabeled target data (semi-supervised learning)? One way to think about it is as follows.

In supervised learning, we have three components: features, instances, and parameters. Given some feature representation, we learn parameters from instances. If we cannot use unlabeled target data to correct bias, we can *throw away* components rather than collect more data. The idea is that, instead of transferring all our features, source instances, and parameters, when learning a model for the target domain, we selectively transfer only some features, only some instances, or only some parameters. Intuitively, we want to throw away components that are source-specific.

Our focus in this chapter will be on approaches assuming a bias in $P(\mathbf{x})$ and focusing on either features or instances. In the next chapter we consider the more difficult scenario of learning under an unknown bias, i.e., where the target distribution is unknown.

4.1   SEMI-SUPERVISED LEARNING AS TRANSFER LEARNING

When we evaluated our semi-supervised learning algorithms in Chapter 3 we did so on domain adaptation problems. Semi-supervised learning algorithms are often used to try to correct bias in training data. Semi-supervised learning algorithms typically assume data is sampled i.i.d. at random, but exploit the marginal distribution of unlabeled data. If the unlabeled data is sampled from unbiased data (the target distribution), semi-supervised learning can be used to automatically correct bias in the training data.

🛑Of course, the applicability of semi-supervised methods depends on the expected error of the learner on the target distribution. While semi-supervised methods can correct bias in data that is not identically distributed, if the target distribution diverges much from the source distribution, predictions on unlabeled data may be so error prone that the pseudo-labeled unlabeled data is of little use to us.

Nevertheless, semi-supervised methods have been successfully applied to domain adaptation problems in the NLP literature. The CoNLL 2007 Shared Task on domain adaptation of dependency parsers [99] was won by [114], who used a form of co-training to adapt parsers trained on newspaper articles to parse scientific papers. The Parsing the Web Shared Task [104] was won by [111], who used a product of self-trained experts, inspired by [69].

The sensitivity of semi-supervised methods to bias in data can be illustrated by looking at how performance correlates with KL divergence. We randomly sampled 50 cross-domain document classification problem instances and compared the performance of a Naive Bayes classifier and a self-trained Naive Bayes classifier doing 5 passes over the unlabeled data, pooling 100 data points in each round. The Naive Bayes classifier did slightly better than the self-trained classifier with a macro-average accuracy of 68.8% compared to 68.2% for self-training. It is clear from the individual accuracies that self-training is better on many datasets and, interestingly, there is a very strong correlation difference between the performance of the two systems and KL divergence. The improvement of self-training over Naive Bayes correlates negatively with KL divergence with a Spearman's ρ of -0.45, which is significant ($p \sim 0.001$). We did the same experiment with the perceptron as our base learner, observing an absolute average improvement of 0.3% and a Spearman's ρ of -0.28, which is also significant ($p \sim 0.04$).

Most previous work on structure prediction learning under bias—domain adaptation, in NLP terms—has focused on modifying existing semi-supervised learning algorithms and much of the work on domain adaptation has also assumed small samples of labeled target data. This chapter presents some of the exceptions and applications of transfer learning algorithms to unsupervised domain adaptation, i.e., domain adaptation where we only have unlabeled data from the target domain.

4.2   TRANSFERRING DATA

4.2.1   OUTLIER DETECTION

The notion of outlier detection was introduced when we talked about nearest neighbor editing in Chapter 3. Outlier detection can be seen as transferring subsets of data. Typically, when we talk about outliers we talk about outliers with respect to the source distribution, but, we can also try to detect outliers with respect to the target distribution. This is very similar to importance weighting, discussed below.

The literature on (multi-variate, non-parametric) outlier detection methods usually distinguishes between distance-based and clustering-based techniques. A distance-based technique could, for example, rank outlier candidates by their average distance to their k-nearest neighbors. Clustering-based methods are typically optimized for clustering and only do implicit outlier detection by leaving out small clusters.

Some of the importance weighting experiments reported on in the NLP literature can be classified as outlier detection for bias correction [72, 121].

4.2.2   IMPORTANCE WEIGHTING

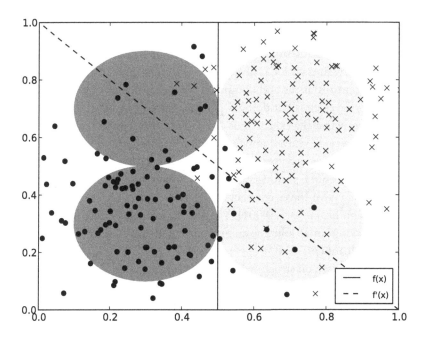

Figure 4.1: Motivation for importance weighting.

Under sampling bias the maximum likelihood estimate does not necessarily provide a good inference. If there is a bias toward one of the classes y in the training data, for example, the maximum likelihood estimate will favor that class and consistently overestimate $\hat{P}(y|\mathbf{x})$. Shimodaira [116] proposes to use a maximum *weighted* (log-)likelihood estimate obtained by maximizing:

$$-\sum_{i=1}^{n} -w_i(\mathbf{x}_i) \log P(y_i|\mathbf{x}_i, \theta) \qquad (4.1)$$

where $w(\cdot)$ is a function that assigns a weight to each of our labeled data points. Shimodaira [116] also shows that the optimal weight function with sufficiently large samples is $P_T(\mathbf{x})/P_S(\mathbf{x})$, where $P_T(\mathbf{x})$ is the density function in the target domain and $P_S(\mathbf{x})$ is the density function in the source domain. The problem, of course, is that density functions typically cannot be computed.

Consider first why, intuitively, importance weighting may lead to better results when our target distribution differs from the source distribution. In the plot in Figure 4.1, the dark gray class is made up of two Gaussian blobs, and so is the light grey class. The dots and crosses represent the sampled data points we have at our disposal. The dashed line represents the model we can learn from this data using a large-margin method, for example. This model has an error rate of 25% wrt. to the overall population and, if the target data is biased favoring the upper dark gray and the lower light gray, the error rate on the target data may be higher than that. If we could somehow assign more weight to the data points from the under-sampled regions, we may end up with something close to the optimal decision boundary (the solid, vertical line).

While we cannot compute a Shimodaira-style importance weight function, several authors have proposed methods to estimate importance weight functions. One such method is to learn **domain models** in order to assign weights to source data points [11, 123, 146]. The idea is, briefly put, to learn a model to distinguish the unlabeled data points from the source distribution from the unlabeled data points from the target distribution. If the learner produces reliable probabilities or scores, each source data point can then be weighted by the model's probability estimate that it was sampled from the target distribution. This is the approach implemented in Figure 4.2. Others have suggested the use of **perplexity given a target domain language model** to weight source distribution data points [121] or focused on small subsets of features where density functions can be adequately estimated [125]. Finally, there are two other important methods that have been proposed in the literature, namely, kernel mean matching [67] and minimizing KL divergence [131].

Kernel mean matching. [67] propose to weight the source data such that the means of the source and target distributions in reproducing Hilbert kernel space are close. The authors cite [57] for the idea of using distribution means to compare samples. The details of this technique are beyond the scope of this book, but we mention it here for completeness.

Minimizing divergence. [131] propose to learn a weight function $w(\cdot)$ that minimizes $KL(w(\mathbf{x})\hat{P}_s(\mathbf{x}), \hat{P}_t(\mathbf{x}))$, where $\hat{P}_s(\mathbf{x})$ is an estimate of the source distribution and $\hat{P}_t(\mathbf{x})$ is an estimate of the target distribution. They cast the problem of finding $w(\cdot)$ as a convex optimization problem, but, we illustrate the technique here by randomly sampling instances of $w(\cdot)$ instead.

Say `options.iterations` is the number of randomly chosen weight functions $w(\cdot)$ you are willing to try. For each iteration we create a new weighted copy of our dataset `X_new`. We can apply any kind of randomly sampled weight function, e.g., from Gaussian or power distributions, to make `X_new` an instance of $w(\mathbf{x})\hat{P}_s(\mathbf{x})$. Here we sample binary weight functions from a binomial distribution to select random subsets of our data points, with `options.rate` being the probability of selecting a feature (drawing 1 rather than 0). We select the one `X_best` that minimizes the KL divergence between source and target data, given the output of some KL divergence estimator KL. See Section 2.1 for implementations of KL.

```
minKL=1.0
for _ in range(options.iterations):
        X_new=np.zeros(X_source.shape)
        weights=np.random.binomial(1,options.rate,size=X_source.shape[0])
        for i in range(X_source.shape[0]):
            X_new[i,:]=X_source[i,:]*weights[i]
        newKL=KL(X_new,X_target)
        if newKL<minKL:
            X_best=X_new
            minKL=newKL
```

👍 Several authors have noted that KL divergence-based weight functions have a tendency to over-fit [31, 130, 144] and some authors have argued Renyi divergence is more appropriate than KL divergence [31]. It is well-known that most standard density estimators converge slowly and that they therefore exhibit considerable variance on small samples. This problem is amplified in high-dimensional spaces, where the density in large areas is necessarily close to 0. Parzen window-based or nearest neighbor-based Jensen-Shannon divergence estimation has been reported to be empirically superior to many other known methods, but still not very robust, in a recent study by Budka et al. [20].

Here we present a simple experiment with importance weighting. The code is given in Figure 4.2. We evaluate importance weighted Naive Bayes on four 20 Newsgroups cross-domain datasets by transforming the dataset to compute instance weights. The baseline Naive Bayes classifier scores 94.76% on this dataset, while the importance-weighted Naive Bayes classifier scores 95.14% with weights estimated by logistic regression.[1] We repeated the experiment on similar datasets using weighted Naive Bayes and weighted perceptron, with importance weights estimated by logistic regression and with 20 passes over data to prevent under-fitting due to down-weighting data. The results are listed in the following table:

Source	Target	NB	IW-NB	Perc.	IW-Perc.
Hockey-IBM	Baseball-Mac	94.76	95.14	86.32	90.28
Hockey-Crypt	Baseball-Electronics	88.99	90.63	76.58	77.22
Guns-Electronics	MidEast-Medicine	72.93	*65.16*	69.69	71.24
Graphics-Misc(Politics)	Windows-Misc(Religion)	94.58	95.36	89.16	89.94

Finally, it has also been proposed to use thresholding [72, 121] or binning in quantiles [31], rather than using the actual weights.[2]

In NLP, importance weighting has been applied to POS tagging [72] and dependency parsing [123, 125] with some success, but, learning a robust weight function can be a challenging task. Some authors have proposed combining several diverse weight functions through voting [125]. See Chapter 5 for more details on using voting to obtain robust systems.

---

[1]Naive Bayes is notoriously bad at predicting probabilities [96], so we use logistic regression instead as our domain learner.
[2]Jiang and Zhai (2007) weight source data by the error of a classifier trained on a small sample of target data, but we do not assume labeled target data here.

```
# datasets
a={1:(['rec.sport.hockey','comp.sys.ibm.pc.hardware'],['rec.sport.baseball',
'comp.sys.mac.hardware']),2:(['rec.sport.hockey','sci.crypt'],['rec.sport.baseball',
'sci.electronics']),3:(['talk.politics.guns','sci.electronics'],
['talk.politics.mideast','sci.med']),4:(['comp.graphics','talk.politics.misc'],
['comp.windows.x','talk.religion.misc'])}
for pair in a:
    S=datasets.fetch_20newsgroups(subset="train",shuffle=True,categories=a[pair][0])
    T=datasets.fetch_20newsgroups(subset="train",shuffle=True,categories=a[pair][1])
    test=datasets.fetch_20newsgroups(subset="test",shuffle=True,categories=a[pair][1])
    # transform data
    y_train,y_test=S.target,test.target
    vectorizer=Vectorizer()
    X_train=vectorizer.fit_transform(S.data)
    X_test=vectorizer.transform(test.data)
    # construct data for domain classifier
    X_dom=vectorizer.transform(S.data+T.data)
    y_dom=[0 for _ in range(len(S.data))] + [1 for _ in range(len(T.data))]
# make target positive class
    y_dom=np.array(y_dom)

    # compute weights of training data being target data
    weights=np.zeros(y_train.shape)
    # fold no. 1 (train on even)
    clf=log()
    clf.fit(X_dom[::2],y_dom[::2])
    # for the odd data points assign probability it's from T
    for i in range(1,X_train.shape[0],2):
        weights[i]=clf.predict_proba(X_dom[i])[0][1]
    # fold no. 2 (train on odd)
    clf.fit(X_dom[1::2],y_dom[1::2])
    # for the even data points assign probability it's from T
    for i in range(0,X_train.shape[0],2):
        weights[i]=clf.predict_proba(X_dom[i])[0][1]

    clf=nb()
    # baseline
    clf.fit(X_train,y_train)
    y_bl=clf.predict(X_test)
    print "bl:," clf.score(X_test,y_test)      # system
    clf.fit(X_train,y_train,sample_weight=weights)
    y_sys=clf.predict(X_test)
    print "sys:," clf.score(X_test,y_test)
```

Figure 4.2: Python code for document classification experiment with importance weighted Naive Bayes.

4.3   TRANSFERRING FEATURES

In the above, we discussed ways to weight the source data to better fit the target data, but, we can also change our feature representations to do so.

4.3.1   CHANGING FEATURE REPRESENTATION TO MINIMIZE DIVERGENCE

We saw in the above that divergence estimation can be used for importance weighting. Divergence estimation can also, in a very similar way, be used for feature selection or feature weighting when learning under bias. Before, we randomly selected instances or weight functions over instances by factoring vectors of random weights into the rows of our datasets and then computed the divergence of target data and the reweighted source sample. Instead of multiplying rows with random [0, 1]-floats, we now multiply the random vectors into our columns instead, downweighting or removing features from our dataset. Note that these two approaches to learning under bias are easily combined, if we draw two random vectors in each iteration.

```
minKL=1.0
for _ in range(options.iterations):
        X_new=np.zeros(X_source.shape)
        weights1=np.random.binomial(1,options.rate,size=X_source.shape[0])
        weights2=np.random.binomial(1,options.rate,size=X_source.shape[1])
        for i in range(X_source.shape[0]):
            X_new[i,:]=X_source[i,:]*weights[i]
        for i in range(X_source.shape[1]):
            X_new[:,i]=X_source[:,i]*weights2[i]
        newKL=KL(X_new,X_target)
        if newKL<minKL:
            X_best=X_new
            minKL=newKL
```

This code, weighting both features and instances, was used in the experiments reported in Figure 4.3, setting the deletion rate to 0.9. We see a small improvement on one problem instance, big improvements on two, and a big loss on the last instance. Note again that, rather than changing the distribution of the data by considering only subspaces, we can also apply weight functions sampled from some set of natural distributions, e.g., Gaussian or power distributions.

Source	Target	Perc.	KL-Perc.
Hockey-IBM	Baseball-Mac	83.25	83.89
Hockey-Crypt	Baseball-Electronics	55.57	70.00
Guns-Electronics	MidEast-Medicine	75.39	58.03
Graphics-Misc(Politics)	Windows-Misc(Religion)	55.73	73.53

Figure 4.3: Comparison of supervised perceptron and minimizing KL divergence in 50 random subspaces, selecting 50 best features with χ^2.

4.3.2 STRUCTURAL CORRESPONDENCE LEARNING

Structural correspondence learning [13] does not fit our taxonomy of domain adaptation strategies above. It builds on the idea that, while we can drop harmful or irrelevant features (e.g., by minimizing divergence between source and target data), we should also be able to introduce features specific to the target data by aligning them to known features. On the other hand, this is similar to clusters-as-features, where word clusters are used to bridge source and target features. The approach is used by [8], except they replace KL divergence with a more sophisticated divergence measure called $\mathcal{A}$-distance.

Consider, for example, the problem of distinguishing between Usenet posts about sports and Usenet posts about vehicles. If we train a model on posts about baseball and motorcycles and evaluate our model on hockey and cars, we will probably not have any support for the feature "puck." This feature, however, would have been extremely informative. While we do not observe this feature in our labeled data, it may concur with known informative features in unlabeled target data, e.g., "score" or "goal." [13] align unknown features to known informative features by training classifiers using unlabeled target data to predict the occurrence of the known informative features, e.g., "score" or "goal." Good features for predicting the word "goal" are then used to augment the learned source domain model. Note that structural correspondence learning has similarities to semi-supervised approaches [5] and depends on the expected error rate of the intermediate classifiers predicting the occurrence of known informative features.

4.4 TRANSFERRING PARAMETERS

Our last option is to drop parameters in our model. Note that in lazy learning our data points *are* our parameters, but in Naive Bayes we can transfer probabilities and in perceptron learning we can transfer weights. If, for example, we can assume that $P_s(y) \sim P_t(y)$, but expect a bias in $P_s(\mathbf{x})$ or $P_s(y \mid \mathbf{x})$, it makes sense to transfer the prior probabilities from our learned model and learn the remaining parameters in a weakly supervised or unsupervised fashion [24], e.g., using EM initialized by prior probabilities estimated using labeled source data. In a similar way we may know the likelihood of some features (that transfer across domains) and we can use them as soft constraints or as terms in our objective function assigning scores to model expectations [46]. We will not explore such directions further here.

CHAPTER 5

Learning under Unknown Bias

The assumption that a large pool of unlabeled data is available from a relatively homogeneous target domain holds only if the target domain is known in advance. In a lot of applications of NLP, this is not the case. When we design publicly available software such as the Stanford Parser, or when we set up online services such as Google Translate, we do not know much about the input in advance. A user will apply the Stanford Parser to any kind of text from any textual domain and expect it to do well. Recent work has extended domain adaptation with domain *identification* [45, 87], but, this still requires that we know the possible domains in advance and are able to relate each instance to one of them, and in many cases we do not. If the possible target domains are *not* known in advance, the transfer learning problem reduces to the problem of learning robust models that are as insensitive as possible to domain shifts. This is the problem considered in this chapter.

We first show how work in adversarial learning, i.e., studies of learning in the presence of an adversary that corrupts data points, labels, or models, can help us achieve better results on new unknown domains and when data is biased in ways we cannot estimate by pooling large volumes of unlabeled data. We then give a brief introduction to ensemble learning and meta-learning, which are orthogonal approaches to the robust learning problem.

5.1 ADVERSARIAL LEARNING

First, let us step back a bit. The main reason for performance drops, when evaluating NLP models on out-of-domain data with a significant bias in $P(\mathbf{x})$, is often said to be out-of-vocabulary (OOV) effects [12, 38]. OOV effects lead to bias in $P(\mathbf{x})$. Several techniques for reducing OOV effects have been introduced in the literature, including spelling expansion, morphological expansion, dictionary term expansion, proper name transliteration, correlation analysis, and word clustering [12, 38, 59, 135]. Spelling expansion may, for example, be useful when the domain shift also introduces a shift in style, e.g., leading to occurrences of *coz* rather than *because* or triple exclamation marks rather than just one. Correlation analysis may be interesting in datasets such as 20 Newsgroups where different words may indicate, say, that the topic is sports across domains, e.g., *bat* and *puck*. These techniques, being far from perfect, introduce noise and cannot solve the problem completely.

The sudden absence of known indicative features may hurt performance considerably. In the perceptron learning algorithm, for example, we learn a weight vector that classifies our training data correctly. In theory we can learn a model that only assigns weight to a single feature if that is enough to classify the training data correctly. If we do not see this feature at test time, we will assign all test examples to the same class. To see this, consider the following dataset:

y	x_1	x_2	x_3
1	1	0	0
0	0	1	0
1	1	0	1
1	0	0	1

In this example features x_1 and x_3 are supposed to be indicative of positive class, while the feature x_2 is indicative of negative class. The perceptron (with $\alpha = 0.1$), however, converges after seeing a single data point with model $\langle .1, 0, 0, -.1 \rangle$, classifying all data points with $x_1 = 1$ as positive, and everything else as negative. However, say x_1 is a word that will never occur in the target domain. Its absence is therefore not indicative of negative class. The test example is wrongly classified as negative, because we never updated the weight associated with feature x_3. The feature, which is weakly correlated with x_1, was "swamped" by the more indicative feature [133].

OOV effects can also lead more advanced algorithms to perform suboptimally, since the best decision boundary in n dimensions is not necessarily the best boundary in $m < n$ dimensions. Consider the plot in Figure 5.1, for illustration. The dataset was sampled at random from two Gaussians. The solid line with no stars (2d-fit) is the SVM fit in two dimensions, while the dashed line is what that fit amounts to if the feature x is missing in the target. The solid line with stars (1d-fit) is our fit if we could predict the missing feature, training a SVM only with the y feature. The 1d-fit decision boundary only misclassifies a single data point compared to the original fit, which misclassifies more than 15 negatives with the x feature missing.

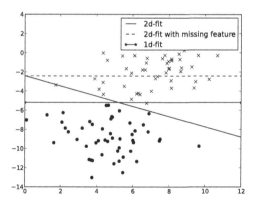

Figure 5.1: Optimal decision boundary is not optimal when one dimension is removed.

The plot in Figure 5.1 shows that the best fit in m dimensions is often not the best in $< m$ dimensions. Consequently, if we think there is a risk that features will be missing in the target, finding the best fit in m dimensions is not necessarily the best we can do. Of course we do not know what features will be missing in advance. The intuition in this paper is that we may obtain more robust decision boundaries by minimizing loss over a set of possible feature deletions.

Adversarial learning [9, 40, 54] is often used in security-related systems. A security-related system may, for example, receive signals from a 100 sensors, but still needs to perform at a certain level, even if some sensors fail to submit signals to the system. The analogy in document classification is that reasonable performance is expected even when some features are not available in the target domain. In adversarial learning, we simulate this scenario by letting an adversary randomly block the signals, i.e., corrupt our data by removing features. However, while worst-case performance is typically important in security-related systems, we will be interested in average-case performance. This means that while most applications of adversarial learning focus on minimizing worst-case loss, the algorithm presented here will give us an approximation of the solution minimizing loss over all or some pre-defined set of possible corruptions of our data.

Of course we are not really interested in performance under all possible corruptions of our data. We would not expect our model to do well with no features at all, for example. In security-related systems, the adversary is typically restricted to remove at most k features from the data, and we will make a similar assumption here.

1: $X = \{\langle y_i, \mathbf{x}_i \rangle\}_{i=1}^N$
2: $\mathbf{w}^0 = 0, \mathbf{v} = 0, i = 0$
3: **for** $k \in K$ **do**
4:   **for** $n \in N$ **do**
5:     $\xi \leftarrow$ **random.binomial**$(1, d, M)$
6:     **if** sign$(\mathbf{w} \cdot \mathbf{x} \circ \xi) \neq y_n$ **then**
7:       $\mathbf{w}^{i+1} \leftarrow$ **update**$(\mathbf{w}^i)$
8:       $i \leftarrow i + 1$
9:     **end if**
10:     $\mathbf{v} \leftarrow \mathbf{v} + \mathbf{w}^i$
11:   **end for**
12: **end for**
13: **return** $\mathbf{w} = \mathbf{v}/(N \times K)$

Figure 5.2: Adversarial online learning.

This approach to learning under unknown bias can be applied to any linear model and we present the general form in Figure 5.2. For each data point $\mathbf{x}_i$, we randomly draw ξ from the set of binary vectors of length M with probability d of scalars being 1. The parameter d will be called the deletion rate. As usual, we update our models if sign$(\mathbf{w} \cdot \mathbf{x} \circ \xi \neq y_n$. The weights of the K models are averaged to minimize the average expected loss in random subspaces. The adversarial learning variant of the perceptron (AL-P) is obtained by replacing line 8 in Figure 5.2 with the perceptron update and by returning $\mathbf{w}^{N \times K}$, rather than the averaged model. The application of AL-P to an artificial two-dimensional dataset in Figure 5.3 (the solid line) illustrates how AL-P can lead to very different decision boundaries than the regular perceptron (the black dashed line). The red dashed lines are the subspace decision boundaries.

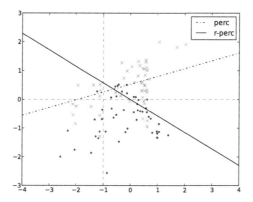

Figure 5.3: Adversarial learning for perceptron on artificial data.

Adversarial learning works well for cross-domain document classification. If we set the deletion rate to 0.9, the adversarial perceptron (AL-P) leads to an 11% error reduction over the standard perceptron on 25 randomly extracted datasets from the 20 Newsgroups [124]. Adversarial learning has also been successfully applied to POS tagging [124]. Interestingly, the same approach does not work as well for dependency parsing. Figure 5.4 presents some results applying the same technique to the transition-based EasyFirst (EP) parser [55] and the graph-based Mate parser [15] with default parameters. The reason probably is that dependency parsers are less sensitive to OOV effects, because they often rely on very informative POS features.

	POS	EP	Mate
EWT-Answers	3.1%	2.4%	0.8%
EWT-Newsgroups	3.3%	1.6%	0.2%
EWT-Reviews	2.8%	0.3%	1.1%
EWT-Weblogs	4.7%	-0.3%	0.4%

Figure 5.4: Adversarial learning error reductions on POS tagging and dependency parsing.

Implementing this kind of adversarial learning in Python is easy. In our from-scratch implementation of the perceptron in Figure 2.7 in Chapter 2 we built the data points in the following line:

```
d=[y[n]]+[X[n,j] for j in range(X.shape[1])]+[-1]
```

This can be replaced by:

```
select=np.random.binomial(1,0.9,size=X.shape[0])
d=[y[n]]+[X[n,j]*select[j] for j in range(X.shape[1])]+[-1]
```

which would randomly remove about 10% of all features. An alternative, if you want to stick to SkLearn, is to copy the training data (10 times if you planned to do 10 iterations), randomly remove features, and just do a single pass over the data.

Adversarial learning can be seen as a form of regularization [40] and is related to drop-out in deep belief networks [66]. See Brückner et al. [19] for a game-theoretic interpretation of adversarial learning.

5.2   ENSEMBLE-BASED METHODS AND META-LEARNING

Ensemble-based learning refers to learning algorithms that exploit many, often very diverse classifiers at the same time. Co-training and tri-training, discussed in Chapter 3, can be said to be ensemble-based semi-supervised learning algorithms. Many researchers working on domain adaptation problems in NLP have successfully combined semi-supervised approaches with ensemble-based learning [69, 87], providing more robust models when data is biased.

The simplest form of ensemble-based learning is **voting**. The intuition is that all supervised learners exhibit some variance (i.e., sensitivity to data sampling) and, when data is biased, learners may learn very different models. The variance can be reduced by combining models. One way to combine n classifiers each taking a guess on $\mathbf{x} \to \{0, 1\}$ is to let them vote on the two classes. If m classifiers vote on negative class (0), we make this our prediction if $m > \frac{n}{2}$. Obviously, if we have some reason to trust some classifiers more than others, e.g., because we know how they performed on held-out data, we can take a weighted vote. Voting is quite popular in dependency parsing, where base parsers vote on the individual dependencies, which gives us a matrix of integer-valued weights. Maximum spanning tree algorithms can then be used to single out the well-formed dependency tree with the maximum number of votes [60, 113]. Voting was also used in [4] to make condensed nearest neighbor (Section 3.3.3) more robust, initializing the ensemble members differently.

A **product of experts** is similar in spirit to weighted voting. In a product of experts, each classifier contributes with its confidence in assigning the labels 0 and 1. If our classifiers are probabilistic, a classifier c's confidence in labeling $\mathbf{x}$, with the label 0 is $P_c(0|\mathbf{x})$. Each data point $\mathbf{x}$ is then assigned the label $\hat{y}$, with highest sum of probabilities across the ensemble classifiers:

$$\hat{y} = \arg \max \sum_{c \in C} P_c(y|\mathbf{x}) \tag{5.1}$$

Stacked generalization, or simply **stacking**, was first proposed by Wolpert [141]. Stacking is an ensemble-based learning method where multiple weak classifiers are combined in a strong end classifier. The idea is to train the end classifier directly on the predictions of the input classifiers. Say each input classifier c_i with $1 \leq i \leq n$ receives an input $\mathbf{x}$ and outputs a prediction $c_i(\mathbf{x})$. The end classifier c_0 then takes as input $\langle \mathbf{x}, c_1(\mathbf{x}), \ldots, c_n(\mathbf{x}) \rangle$ and outputs a final prediction $c_0(\langle \mathbf{x}, c_1(\mathbf{x}), \ldots, c_n(\mathbf{x}) \rangle)$. Training data is augmented with predictions using cross-validation. In sum, stacking is training a classifier on the output of classifiers. We now present a simple stacking experiment in Python code.

The first thing we need to do is to label our training data with our base learner. This can be done using cross-validation. In SkLearn there is a module devoted to cross-validation. Below y_b0 collects the predictions of a Naive Bayes base learner over five folds.

```
kf=cross_validation.KFold(n=X.shape[0],k=5)
y_b0=[]
for tr_i, te_i in kf:
    b0=nb()
    X_train,X_test=X[tr_i],X[te_i]
    y_train,y_test=y[tr_i],y[te_i]
    b0.fit(X_train,y_train)
    y_b0+=list(b0.predict(X_test))
```

Having labeled the training data by base learner predictions, we can now augment the training data with these predictions. In order to do so we introduce a new matrix X_stacked.

```
X_stacked=np.zeros((X.shape[0],X.shape[1]+1))
for i in range(X.shape[0]):
    for j in range(X.shape[1]):
        X_stacked[i,j]=X[i,j]
    X_stacked[i,-1]=y_b0[i]
```

We then augment the test data with base learner predictions the same way. All there is left is training our stacked classifier on X_stacked and apply it to the augmented test data.

In stacked learning, our end classifier may learn to correct the errors of one or more input classifiers. In **meta-learning**, we try to learn what input classifiers to trust on a given data point. Meta-learning thus relies on the assumptions that some classifiers do better on some of our data points, but others do better on others. The simple meta-learning experiment in Figure 5.5, where we use a perceptron to learn whether to trust a perceptron or a nearest neighbor classifier, gives an accuracy of 77.8%. The perceptron accuracy is a little lower (77.7%), while the nearest neighbor accuracy is 66.8%. The meta-learner (also a perceptron) seems to learn when to trust the perceptron and when to trust the nearest neighbor rule, though the effect is not significant.

```
from sklearn.neighbors import KNeighborsClassifier as L2
from sklearn.linear_model import Perceptron as L1
pair=(['rec.autos','sci.space'],['rec.motorcycles','sci.crypt'])
train=datasets.fetch_20newsgroups(subset="train",shuffle=True,categories=pair[0])
test=datasets.fetch_20newsgroups(subset="test",shuffle=True,categories=pair[1])
y,y_eval=train.target,test.target
vectorizer=feature_extraction.text.TfidfVectorizer()
vectorizer.fit(train.data)
X=vectorizer.transform(train.data)
X_eval=vectorizer.transform(test.data)
kf=cross_validation.KFold(n=X.shape[0],k=10)
y_b0,y_b1,y_gold=[],[],[]
for tr_i, te_i in kf:
    b0,b1=L1(),L2()
    X_train,X_test=X[tr_i],X[te_i]
    y_train,y_test=y[tr_i],y[te_i]
    b0.fit(X_train,y_train)
    y_b0+=list(b0.predict(X_test))
    b1.fit(X_train,y_train)
    y_b1+=list(b1.predict(X_test))
    y_gold+=list(y_test)
nb_right=[1-abs(y_b0[i]-y_gold[i]) for i in range(len(y_gold))]
perc_right=[1-abs(y_b1[i]-y_gold[i]) for i in range(len(y_gold))]
y_meta=[0 if perc_right[i]==1 and nb_right[i]!=1 else 1 for i in range(X.shape[0])]
meta=L1()
meta.fit(X,y_meta)
b0,b1=L1(),L2()
b0.fit(X,y)
b1.fit(X,y)
y_pred=[]
for i in range(X_eval.shape[0]):
    if meta.predict(X_eval[i,:])[0]==1:
        y_pred.append(b0.predict(X_eval[i,:])[0])
    else:
        y_pred.append(b1.predict(X_eval[i,:])[0])
print metrics.zero_one_score(y_eval,y_pred)
print "baselines:"
print b0.score(X_eval,y_eval)
print b1.score(X_eval,y_eval)
```

Figure 5.5: Simple meta-learning experiment.

CHAPTER 6

Evaluating under Bias

6.1 WHAT IS LANGUAGE?

In NLP we often talk about having "a good parser of German" or whether it is harder to parse Chinese than to parse English. In practice, however, we never seem to answer those questions. In order to test whether a parser A is a better parser of German than a parser B, we would, of course, have to evaluate A and B on a representative sample of German, but such samples probably do not exist. Even the big national corpora seem to favor particular types of language, and there is so much individual variation from language user to language user that the idea of being able to sample a representative corpus of a language seems somewhat exotic—when you think about it.

NLP tools and online services such as the Stanford Parser or Google Translate are used for a wide variety of purposes and, therefore, also on very different kinds of data. Some use the Stanford Parser to parse literature, while others use it for processing social media content. The parser, however, was not necessarily evaluated on literature or social media content during development. Still, users typically expect reasonable performance on any natural language input. I think we need to ask ourselves what we, as developers, can do to estimate the effect of a change to our system—not on the labeled test data that happens to be available to us, but on future, still unseen datasets provided by our end users.

The standard approach to significance testing in NLP, in contrast, works as follows: Sample a test set T of some size from your labeled data and evaluate the systems A and B on T. Say A is slightly better than B. Significance is typically computed using paired bootstrap [47] in which we draw bootstrap samples of T of size n (with replacement). The p-value we compute is then the ratio of bootstrap samples where B is better than A. See Berg-Kirkpatrick et al. [10] for a recent survey of significance testing in NLP. The p-value says what the probability is that, if we sampled more test data (i.i.d. at random) from the same distribution, B would be better than A.

In this book we have assumed that data in NLP is always biased. In my view it follows from this that we need to evaluate our classifiers, taggers, and parsers across as many datasets as possible and that, rather than being interested in whether A is significantly better at parsing cooking recipes than B, we should be interested in our confidence that A will do better than B on the next, possibly very different dataset.

All experiments in this book were on cross-domain datasets and, in many cases, we reported average scores over multiple datasets. While I believe this kind of evaluation is more relevant than reporting accuracies on a single in-domain dataset, we still do not say much about how likely it is that A will perform better than B on new datasets. If we assume that the datasets we are evaluating

A and B on are drawn independently and identically at random, a significance test across several datasets (rather than across data points) may answer that question.

Demsar [42] presents motivation for using non-parametric methods, such as the Wilcoxon signed rank test, to estimate significance across datasets. Student's t-test is based on means and, typically, results across datasets are not commensurable. The t-test is also extremely sensitive to outliers. Notice also that usually we do not have enough datasets to do paired bootstrapping across datasets.

In addition, we may be interested in estimating not only the sign of the effect—whether A is better than B—but also, the actual effect size—by how much A is better than B. The effect size may be crucial for balancing the trade-off between performance and computational efficiency. In Section 6.3, we present a brief introduction to meta-analysis—popular in fields such as psychology and medicine. We also present empirical results suggesting that, in some cases, meta-analysis provides better estimates of effect sizes than macro- or micro-averages.

Standard meta-analysis, however, makes an important assumption, namely that the effect sizes are normally distributed. In order to make sure that effects are commensurable, we can use error reductions as effects, but error reductions do not appear to be normally distributed. In practice, however—at least in the case of cross-domain document classification with 20 Newsgroups—meta-analysis seems superior to macro- or micro-average. Alternatives include non-parametric meta-analysis [65, 136] and more recently proposed parametric methods [119]. Here we limit ourselves to standard meta-analysis.

Meta-analysis, of course, also relies on the assumptions that datasets are drawn i.i.d. at random. If we *cannot* make that assumption, we need to do something else to predict effect size. One thing we can do is look at what dataset characteristics our performance gains seem to depend on. In Figure 2.9 at page 27, for example, we presented a comparison of supervised learning algorithms and looked at how performance correlated with KL divergence. If we can establish significant correlations between data characteristics and performance, we may be able to say something about whether A will perform better than B on new datasets with specific characteristics, even in the absence of a representative sample of datasets. This option is briefly discussed in Section 6.4.

6.2   SIGNIFICANCE ACROSS CORPORA

Demsar [42] points out that running a paired t-test over the results of two classifiers on m datasets to test whether the average difference in their performance is significantly different from zero, has a number of weaknesses: (a) scores need to be commensurable for averaging to make sense; (b) unless we have about thirty or more datasets, the performances across datasets need to be normally distributed, which they probably are not; finally, (c) the t-test is very sensitive to outliers. Demsar [42] instead recommends doing a Wilcoxon signed rank test over multiple datasets. Scipy includes this significance test in the module `stats`. The function `stats.wilcoxon` simply takes two lists or arrays of accuracies, those of your baseline and those of your system, and outputs a p-value. A

Wilcoxon signed rank test over multiple datasets tells us if we are justified in saying that our systems are unlikely to be worse than our baselines, *on average*.

6.3 META-ANALYSIS

Meta-analysis is the statistical analysis of effect size across several studies and is very popular in fields such as psychology or medicine. Meta-analysis has not been applied very often to NLP. In NLP, most people work on applying *new* methods to *old* datasets, and meta-analysis is designed to analyze series of studies applying *old* methods to *new* datasets, e.g., running the same experiments on new samples of subjects. However, meta-analysis *is* applicable to experiments with multiple datasets.

In psychology or medicine you often see studies running similar experiments on different samples, with very different results. Meta-analysis stems from the observation that, if we want to estimate an effect from a large set of studies, the average effect across all the studies will put too much weight on results obtained in small or low-quality experiments in which you typically see more variance. The most popular approaches to meta-analysis are the fixed effects and the random effects model [16]. The fixed effects model is applicable when you assume the individual studies estimate the same effect size. If you cannot make that assumption because the studies may differ in various aspects, leading the within-study estimates to be estimates of slightly different effect sizes, you need to use the random effects model. Both approaches to meta-analysis are parametric and rely on the effect sizes to be normally distributed.

In the **fixed effects model** we weight the effect sizes $T_1, \ldots, T_M$—or accuracies, in our case—by something related to sample size, but, rather than doing a simple micro-average, we weight each of our results by the inverse of the variance v_i in the study. The combined effect size T is then:

$$\hat{T} = \frac{\sum_{i \geq 1}^{M} w_i T_i}{\sum_{i \geq 1}^{M} w_i} \tag{6.1}$$

The variance of the combined effect is now:

$$v = \frac{1}{\sum_{i \geq 1}^{M} w_i} \tag{6.2}$$

and the 95% confidence interval is then:

$$\hat{T} \pm 1.96\sqrt{v} \tag{6.3}$$

In the **random effects model** we replace the variance v_i with the variance plus between-studies variance τ^2:

$$\tau^2 = \frac{\sum_{i \geq 1}^{k} w_i T_i^2 - \frac{(\sum_{i \geq 1}^{k} w_i T_i)^2}{\sum_{i \geq 1}^{k} w_i} - df}{\sum_{i \geq 1}^{k} w_i - \frac{\sum_{i \geq 1}^{k} w_i^2}{\sum_{i \geq 1}^{k} w_i}} \tag{6.4}$$

with degree of freedom $df = N - 1$, except all negative values are replaced by 0.

Let us try to compute the 95% confidence interval for a series of 25 randomly extracted cross-domain problem instances from 20 Newsgroups. The code is presented in Figure 6.1. Note that we need to use a random effects model in this case, since the problem instances have very different characteristics. The function `TwentyNewsgroups` returns a random problem instance. Note, also, that we cannot use the variance of the 1-0 loss as is, but, use bootstrap sampling with replacement to estimate the within-study variance. The within-study variance in the fixed effects model is `v=1/sum(_r3)`. While the fixed effects model produces a narrow confidence interval, the random effects model is more conservative.

```
_r1,_r2,_r3=[],[],[]

for _ in range(25):
    X_train,y_train,X_test,y_test=TwentyNewsgroups()

    clf=perc()
    clf.fit(X_train,y_train)
    y_hat=clf.predict(X_test)
    r1=metrics.zero_one_score(y_test,y_hat)
    _var=[]
    for _ in range(50):
        sample=np.random.randint(0,y_test.shape[0],size=y_test.shape[0])
        _var.append(metrics.zero_one_score(y_test[sample],y_hat[sample]))
    w_i=1/np.array(_var).var()
    _r1.append(r1)
    _r2.append(w_i*r1)
    _r3.append(w_i)

T=sum(_r2)/sum(_r3)

thau_squared=(sum(_r2_squared)-((sum(_r2)**2)/sum(_r3))-24)/\
(sum(_r3)-(sum (_r3_squared)/(sum(_r3))))
if thau_squared < 0:
    thau_squared=0
_r4=[]
for old_w_i in _r3:
    _r4.append(1/old_w_i+thau_squared)
v=1/sum(_r4)

print "macro-av.:," sum(_r1)/len(_r1)
print "weighted mean:," T
print "95% conf.int.:", T-1.96*sqrt(v) "<-->", T+1.96*sqrt(v)
```

Figure 6.1: Code for computing 95% confidence interval of accuracy using a random effects model.

We can use meta-analysis to estimate effect sizes. The effect sizes need to be commensurable, so here, we try to estimate error reductions instead of estimating absolute improvements over the baseline. In a fixed effects model, the 95% confidence interval estimated on 25 randomly extracted problem instances that Naive Bayes is better than perceptron is [3.9%, 5.2%]. The weighted mean is 4.6% and the macro-average is 3.9%. Using a random effects model on the same 25 datasets, the 95% confidence interval becomes [−6.5%, 6.6%]. This, I believe, is a more realistic estimate, because of the heterogeneous nature of our data. This is also supported by the observation that on a second run the average improvement Δ was only 1.3% and the weighted mean only 1.2%. It is easier to estimate error reductions, since they vary less across datasets. ☺ Note, however, that we still rely on the effect sizes being roughly normally distributed.

Figure 6.2 presents a comparison of meta-analysis and macro-average by their ability to predict the error reductions of a Naive Bayes learner over a perceptron model on new datasets. In each experiment, we randomly select k datasets and estimate the true effect size using macro-average, a fixed effects model, a random effects model, and a corrected random effects model. Since our datasets are balanced, micro-average will be almost identical to macro-average. In order to estimate the within-study variance, we take 50 paired bootstrap samples of the system outputs. We evaluate our estimates against the observed average effect across five new randomly extracted datasets. For each k, we repeat the experiment 20 times and report average error. We vary k to see how many observations are needed for our estimates to be reliable. We note that meta-analysis provides much better estimates than macro-averages across the board.

	macro-av	fixed	random
$k = 5$			
err.	−0.1656	**−0.0350**	−0.0428
p-value	–	< 0.001	< 0.001
$k = 10$			
err.	−0.1402	**−0.0329**	−0.0413
p-value	–	< 0.001	< 0.001
$k = 15$			
err.	−0.0809	−0.0799	−0.0804
p-value	–	< 0.001	< 0.001

Figure 6.2: Using macro-average and meta-analysis to predict error reductions on document classification datasets based on k observations. The scores are averages across 20 experiments. The p-values were computed using Wilcoxon signed rank tests.

6.4 PERFORMANCE AND DATA CHARACTERISTICS

The Danish physicist Niels Bohr once said that predictions are difficult—especially about the future. In order for macro-averages or weighted means to be meaningful predictions about the future, our datasets need to be sampled i.i.d. at random. Our datasets probably are not. In order to predict the performance of algorithms A and B on future datasets, we can instead try to learn correlations between dataset characteristics and the algorithms' performance.

Say we are interested in how the performance of Naive Bayes correlates with KL divergence, and we will use a fixed effects model to compute a weighted mean and a 95% confidence interval over 10 randomly extracted datasets. The within-study variance is estimated as the variance in performance over 50 bootstrap samples. The macro-average of the correlation coefficients in our first run was -0.088, but the weighted mean is -0.124. The 95% confidence interval is $[-0.131, -0.117]$. The macro-average for the perceptron on the same 10 datasets was -0.075 and the weighted mean was -0.0739 with 95% confidence interval $[-0.082, -0.066]$.

Correlating performance with dataset characteristics gives us a better understanding of how our methods work. In particular, we can see how important assumptions, such as low-density separation or the single cluster assumption, are for performance. The dataset characteristics can also be used for meta-learning (Section 5.2), as well as for developing better methods for learning under bias. If performance correlates with a particular divergence measure, we can try to minimize divergence between source and target relative to that measure.

6.5   DOWN-STREAM EVALUATION

🛑 It is important to remember that, while researchers developing learning algorithms for POS tagging and dependency parsing seem obsessed with accuracies, POS sequences or dependency structures have no interest on their own. The accuracies reported in the literature are only interesting insofar as they correlate with the usefulness of the structures predicted by our systems.

Fortunately, POS sequences and dependency structures *are* useful in many applications. Using POS tagging has improved performance in, for example, sentence boundary detection [101], word completion [49], and machine translation [107], while dependency parsing has been reported to improve performance in sentiment analysis [74], machine translation [48, 52, 142], and many other applications. Ideally, however, all positive results in the POS tagging and parsing literature should be backed up by results showing that increased accuracies also lead to better performance down the stream. For recent papers on down-stream evaluation of parsers, see [48, 61, 93, 94, 145].

Bibliography

List of Abbreviations

AAAI	=	*Proceedings of the National Conference on Artificial Intelligence (until 2006) or the Proceedings of the AAAI Conference on Artificial Intelligence (2007 on).*
ACL	=	*Proceedings of the Annual Meeting of the Association for Computational Linguistics.*
ACL-IJCNLP	=	*Proceedings of the Annual Meeting of the Association for Computational Linguistics and the International Joint Conference on Natural Language Processing.*
CICLing	=	*Proceedings of the Conference on Intelligent Text Processing and Computational Linguistics.*
COLING	=	*Proceedings of the International Conference on Computational Linguistics.*
COLT	=	*Proceedings of the Conference on Learning Theory.*
CoNLL	=	*Proceedings of the Conference on Computational Natural Language Learning.*
EACL	=	*Proceedings of the Conference of the Conference of the Chapter of the Association for Computational Linguistics.*
ECML	=	*Proceedings of the European Conference on Machine Learning and Principles and Practice of Knowledge Discovery in Databases.*
EMNLP	=	*Proceedings of the Conference on Empirical Methods in Natural Language Processing.*
EMNLP-CoNLL	=	*Proceedings of the Conference on Empirical Methods in Natural Language Processing and the Conference on Computational Natural Language Learning.*
HLT-EMNLP	=	*EMNLP.*
HLT-NAACL	=	*NAACL.*
ICML	=	*Proceedings of the International Conference on Machine Learning.*
IWPT	=	*Proceedings of the International Conference on Parsing Technologies.*
JMLR	=	*Journal of Machine Learning Research.*
KDD	=	*Proceedings of the ACM SIGKDD Conference on Knowledge Discovery and Data Mining.*
LREC	=	*Proceedings of the Language Resources and Evaluation Conference.*
NAACL and NAACL-HLT	=	*Proceedings of the Conference of the North American Chapter of the Association for Computational Linguistics: Human Language Technologies.*
NIPS	=	*Proceedings of the Conference on Neural Information Processing Systems.*
NLPRS	=	*Proceedings of the Natural Language Processing Pacific Rim Symposium.*

[1] Steven Abney. *Semi-supervised learning for computational linguistics*. Chapman & Hall, 2008. 41, 43, 49

[2] Steven Abney, Park Avenue, and Florham Park. Bootstrapping. In *ACL*, pages 360–367, 2002. 46

[3] Steven Abney, Robert Schapire, and Yoram Singer. Boosting applied to tagging and PP-attachment. In *EMNLP*, 1999. 29

[4] Ethem Alpaydin. Voting over multiple condensed nearest neighbors. *Artificial Intelligence Review*, 11:115–132, 1997. DOI: 10.1023/A:1006563312922 53, 71

[5] Rie Ando and Tong Zhang. A framework for learning predictive structure from multiple tasks and unlabeled data. *Journal of Machine Learning Research*, 6:1817–1853, 2005. 42, 65

[6] Maria-Florina Balcan, Avrim Blum, and Ke Yang. Co-training and expansion: towards bridging theory and practice. In *NIPS*, 2004. 46

[7] Leonard Baum and Ted Petrie. Statistical inference fror probabilistic functions of finite state Markov chains. *Annals of Mathematical Statistics*, 37:1554–1563, 1966. DOI: 10.1214/aoms/1177699147 35

[8] Shai Ben-David, John Blitzer, Koby Crammer, and Fernando Pereira. Analysis of representations for domain adaptation. In *NIPS*, 2007. DOI: 10.1214/aoms/1177699147 65

[9] Aharon Ben-Tal and Arkadi Nemirovski. Robust convex optimization. *Mathematics of Operations Research*, 23(4), 1998. DOI: 10.1287/moor.23.4.769 69

[10] Taylor Berg-Kirkpatrick, David Burkett, and Dan Klein. An empirical investigation of statistical significance in NLP. In *EMNLP*, 2012. 75

[11] Steffen Bickel and Tobias Scheffer. Dirichlet-enhanced spam filtering based on biased samples. In *NIPS*, 2007. 61

[12] John Blitzer, Mark Dredze, and Fernando Pereira. Biographies, Bollywood, boom-boxes and blenders: Domain adaptation for sentiment classification. In *ACL*, 2007. 67

[13] John Blitzer, Ryan McDonald, and Fernando Pereira. Domain adaptation with structural correspondence learning. In *EMNLP*, 2006. DOI: 10.3115/1610075.1610094 65

[14] Avrim Blum and Tom Mitchell. Combining labeled and unlabeled data with co-training. In *COLT*, 1998. DOI: 10.1145/279943.279962 45, 46

[15] Bernd Bohnet. Top accuracy and fast dependency parsing is not a contradiction. In *COLING*, 2010. 70

[16] M. Borenstein, L. Hedges, P. Higgins, and H. Rothstein. *Introduction to meta-analysis*. John Wiley, 2009. DOI: 10.1002/9780470743386 77

[17] Leo Breiman. Bagging predictors. *Machine Learning*, 24(2):123–140, 1996. DOI: 10.1023/A:1018054314350 53

[18] Peter Brown, Vincent Della Pietra, Stephan Della Pietra, and Robert Mercer. The mathematics of statistical machine translation: parameter estimation. *Computational Linguistics*, 19(2):263–311, 1993. 36

[19] Michael Brückner, Christian Kanzow, and Tobias Scheffer. Static prediction games for adversarial learning problems. In *JMLR*, 2012. 71

[20] Marcin Budka, Bogdan Gabrys, and Katarzyna Musial. On accuracy of pdf divergence estimators and their applicability to representative sampling. *Entropy*, 13:1229–1126, 2011. DOI: 10.3390/e13071229 62

[21] Rich Caruana and Alexandru Niculescu-Mizil. An empirical comparison of supervised learning algorithms. In *ICML*, 2006. DOI: 10.1145/1143844.1143865 28

[22] Giovanni Cavallanti, Nicolò Cesa-Bianchi, and Claudio Gentile. Tracking the best hyperplane with a simple budget perceptron. In *COLT*, 2006. DOI: 10.1007/11776420_36 29

[23] Eugene Charniak, Curtis Hendrickson, Neil Jacobson, and Mike Perkowitz. Equations for part-of-speech tagging. In *AAAI*, 1993. 35

[24] Ciprian Chelba and Alex Acero. Adaptation of maximum entropy capitalizer. In *EMNLP*, 2004. 65

[25] Bo Chen, Wai Lam, Ivor Tsang, and Tak-Lam Wong. Extracting discriminative concepts for domain adaptation in text mining. In *KDD*, 2009. DOI: 10.1145/1557019.1557045 5

[26] Minmin Chen, Killiang Weinberger, and John Blitzer. Co-training for domain adaptation. In *NIPS*, 2011. 46

[27] Ken Church. A stochastic parts program and noun phrase parser for unrestricted text. In *ACL*, 1988. DOI: 10.3115/974235.974260 35

[28] Stephen Clark, James Curran, and Mike Osborne. Bootstrapping POS taggers using unlabeled data. In *CoNLL*, Edmonton, Canada, 2003. DOI: 10.3115/1119176.1119183 43, 46

[29] Shay Cohen, Carlos Rodriguez, and Giorgio Satta. Exact inference for generative probabilistic non-projective dependency parsing. In *EMNLP*, 2011. 39

[30] Michael Collins. Discriminative training methods for Hidden Markov Models. In *EMNLP*, 2002. DOI: 10.3115/1118693.1118694 25, 35, 37

[31] Corinna Cortes, Yishay Mansour, and Mehryar Mohri. Learning bounds for importance weighting. In *NIPS*, 2010. 62

[32] Corinna Cortes and Vladimir Vapnik. Support-vector networks. *Machine Learning*, 20(3):273–297, 1995. DOI: 10.1023/A:1022627411411 25

[33] Koby Crammer, Ofer Dekel, Joseph Keshet, Shai Shalev-Shwartz, and Yoram Singer. Online passive-agressive algorithms. *Journal of Machine Learning Research*, 7:551–585, 2006. 25

[34] Koby Crammer, A Kulesza, and Mark Dredze. Adaptive regularization of weighted vectors. In *NIPS*, 2009. DOI: 10.1007/s10994-013-5327-x 25

[35] Koby Crammer and Yoram Singer. Ultraconservative algorithms for multiclass problems. In *JMLR*, 2003. DOI: 10.1162/jmlr.2003.3.4-5.951 25, 30

[36] Walter Daelemans, Antal Van Den Bosch, and Jakub Zavrel. Forgetting exceptions is harmful in language learning. *Machine Learning*, 34(1–3):11–41, 1999. DOI: 10.1023/A:1007585615670 53

[37] Walter Daelemans, Antal van den Bosch, and Ton Weijters. IGTree: using trees for compression and classification in lazy learning algorithms. *Artificial Intelligence Review*, 11:407–423, 1997. DOI: 10.1023/A:1006506017891 52

[38] Hal Daumé and Jagadeesh Jagarlamudi. Domain adaptation for machine translation by mining unseen words. In *ACL*, 2011. 67

[39] Ofer Dekel, Shai Shalev-Shwartz, and Yoram Singer. The forgetron: a kernel-based perceptron on a fixed budget. In *NIPS*, 2005. DOI: 10.1137/060666998 25

[40] Ofer Dekel and Ohad Shamir. Learning to classify with missing and corrupted features. In *ICML*, 2008. DOI: 10.1145/1390156.1390184 69, 71

[41] Arthur Dempster, Nan Laird, and Donald Rubin. Maximum likelihood from incomplete data via the EM algorithm. *Journal of the Royal Statistical Society*, 39(1):1–38, 1977. 49

[42] Janez Demsar. Statistical comparisons of classifiers over multiple data sets. *Journal of Machine Learning Research*, 7:1–30, 2006. 76

[43] P. Domingos and M. Pazzani. On the optimality of the simple Bayesian classifier under zero-one loss. *Machine Learning*, 29:103–130, 1997. DOI: 10.1023/A:1007413511361 22

[44] Mark Dredze, Koby Crammer, and Fernando Pereira. Confidence-weighted linear classification. In *ICML*, 2008. DOI: 10.1145/1390156.1390190 25

[45] Mark Dredze, Tim Oates, and Christine Piatko. We're not in Kansas anymore: detecting domain changes in streams. In *EMNLP*, 2010. 67

[46] Gregory Druck, Gideon Mann, and Andrew McCallum. Semi-supervised learning of dependency parsers using generalized expectation criteria. In *ACL-IJCNLP*, 2009. DOI: 10.3115/1687878.1687930 65

[47] Bradley Efron and Robert Tibshirani. *An introduction to the bootstrap*. Chapman & Hall, Boca Raton, FL, 1993. 75

[48] Jakob Elming, Anders Johannsen, Sigrid Klerke, Emanuele Lapponi, Hector Martinez Alonso, and Anders Søgaard. Down-stream effects of tree-to-dependency conversions. In *NAACL*, 2013. 80

[49] Afsaneh Fazly and Graeme Hirst. Testing the efficacy of part-of-speech information in word completion. In *EACL*, pages 9–16, Budapest, Hungary, 2003. 80

[50] Yoav Freund and Robert Schapire. Large margin classification using the perceptron algorithm. *Machine Learning*, 37:277–296, 1999. DOI: 10.1023/A:1007662407062 25

[51] Jerome Friedman, Trevor Hastie, and Robert Tibshirani. Additive logistic regression: a statistical view of boosting. *Annals of Statistics*, 28(2):337–407, 2000. DOI: 10.1214/aos/1016218223 29

[52] Michel Galley and Christopher Manning. Quadratic-time dependency parsing for machine translation. In *ACL*, 2009. 80

[53] Geoffrey Gates. The reduced nearest neighbor rule. *IEEE Transactions on Information Theory*, 18(3):431–433, 1972. DOI: 10.1109/TIT.1972.1054809 53

[54] Amir Globerson and Sam Roweis. Nightmare at test time: robust learning by feature deletion. In *ICML*, 2006. DOI: 10.1145/1143844.1143889 69

[55] Yoav Goldberg and Michael Elhadad. An efficient algorithm for easy-first non-directional dependency parsing. In *NAACL*, 2010. 70

[56] Sally Goldman and Yan Zhou. Enhancing supervised learning with unlabeled data. In *ICML*, 2000. 46

[57] A Gretton, K Borgwardt, M Rasch, B Schölkolpf, and A Smola. A kernel method for the two-sample problem. In *NIPS*, 2007. 61

[58] Donghai Guan, Weiwei Yuan, Young-Koo Lee, and Sungyoung Lee. Nearest neighbor editing aided by unlabeled data. *Information Sciences*, 179:2273–2282, 1993. DOI: 10.1016/j.ins.2009.02.011 50, 52

[59] Nizar Habash. Four techniques for online handling of out-of-vocabulary words in Arabic-English statistical machine translation. In *ACL*, 2008. 67

[60] Johan Hall, Jens Nilsson, Joakim Nivre, Gülsen Eryigit, Beáta Megyesi, Mattias Nilsson, and Markus Saers. Single malt or blended? In *CoNLL*, 2007. 71

[61] Keith Hall, Ryan McDonald, Jason Katz-Brown, and Michael Ringgaard. Training dependency parsers by jointly optimizing multiple objectives. In *EMNLP*, 2011. 7, 80

[62] David Hand. Classifier technology and illusion of progress. *Statistical Science*, 21(1):1–15, 2006. DOI: 10.1214/088342306000000079 7, 11, 57

[63] David Hand and Keming Yu. Idiot's Bayes – not so stupid after all? *International Statistical Review*, 69:385–398, 2001. DOI: 10.1111/j.1751-5823.2001.tb00465.x 22

[64] Peter Hart. The condensed nearest neighbor rule. *IEEE Transactions on Information Theory*, 14:515–516, 1968. DOI: 10.1109/TIT.1968.1054155 52, 53

[65] Larry Hedges and Ingram Olkin. Nonparametric estimators of effect size in meta-analysis. *Psychological Bulletin*, 96:573–580, 1984. DOI: 10.1037/0033-2909.96.3.573 76

[66] Geoffrey Hinton, N. Srivastava, A. Krizhevsky, I. Sutskever, and R. Salakhutdinov. Improving neural networks by preventing co-adaptation of feature detectors. http://arxiv.org/abs/1207.0580, 2012. 71

[67] Jiayuan Huang, Alexander Smola, Arthur Gretton, Karsten Borgwardt, and Bernhard Schölkopf. Correcting sample bias by unlabeled data. In *NIPS*, 2007. 30, 61

[68] Zhongqiang Huang, Vladimir Eidelman, and Mary Harper. Improving a simple bigram HMM part-of-speech tagger by latent annotation and self-training. In *NAACL-HLT*, 2009. DOI: 10.3115/1620853.1620911 43

[69] Zhongqiang Huang, Mary Harper, and Slav Petrov. Self-training with products of latent variable grammars. In *EMNLP*, 2009. DOI: 10.3115/1699571.1699621 44, 59, 71

[70] Gareth James. Variance and bias for general loss functions. *Machine Learning*, 51:115–135, 2003. DOI: 10.1023/A:1022899518027 17

[71] N. Japkowicz and S. Stephen. The class imbalance problem. *Intelligent Data Analysis*, 6, 2002. 57

[72] Jing Jiang and ChengXiang Zhai. Instance weighting for domain adaptation in NLP. In *ACL*, 2007. 59, 62

[73] Thorsten Joachims. Transductive inference for text classification using support vector machines. In *ICML*, 1999. 41

[74] Mahesh Joshi and Carolyn Penstein-Rose. Generalizing dependency features for opinion mining. In *ACL*, 2009. 80

[75] Jun'ichi Kazama, Yusuke Miyao, and Jun'ichi Tsujii. A maximum entropy tagger with unsupervised hidden Markov models. In *NLPRS*, 2001. 50

[76] Dan Klein and Christopher Manning. Corpus-based induction of syntactic structure: models of dependency and constituency. In *ACL*, 2004. DOI: 10.3115/1218955.1219016 36

[77] Terry Koo, Xavier Carreras, and Michael Collins. Simple semi-supervised dependency parsing. In *ACL*, 2008. 50

[78] Sandra Kübler, Ryan McDonald, and Joakim Nivre. *Dependency parsing*. Morgan & Claypool, 2009. DOI: 10.2200/S00169ED1V01Y200901HLT002 38, 40

[79] John Lafferty, Andrew McCallum, and Fernando Pereira. Conditional random fields: probabilistic models for segmenting and labeling sequence data. In *ICML*, 2001. 37

[80] Ming Li and Zhi-Hua Zhou. Tri-training: exploiting unlabeled data using three classifiers. *IEEE Transactions on Knowledge and Data Engineering*, 17(11):1529–1541, 2005. DOI: 10.1109/TKDE.2005.186 46, 47

[81] Andrew L Maas, Raymond E Daly, Peter T Pham, Dan Huang, Andrew Y Ng, and Christopher Potts. Learning word vectors for sentiment analysis. In *ACL*, 2011. 2

[82] Chris Manning. Part-of-speech tagging from 97% to 100%: Is it time for some linguistics? In *CICLing*, 2011. 7

[83] Chris Manning and Hinrich Schütze. *Foundations of statistical natural language processing*. MIT Press, Cambridge, MA, 1999. 19

[84] Mitchell Marcus, Mary Marcinkiewicz, and Beatrice Santorini. Building a large annotated corpus of English: the Penn Treebank. *Computational Linguistics*, 19(2):313–330, 1993. 4

[85] Stephen Marsland. *Machine learning: an algorithmic perspective*. CRS Press, New Jersey, US, 2008. 14

[86] David McClosky, Eugene Charniak, and Mark Johnson. Effective self-training for parsing. In *HLT-NAACL*, 2006. 44

[87] David McClosky, Eugene Charniak, and Mark Johnson. Automatic domain adaptation for parsing. In *NAACL-HLT*, 2010. 67, 71

[88] Ryan McDonald and Joakim Nivre. Characterizing the errors of data-driven dependency parsers. In *EMNLP-CoNLL*, 2007. 40

[89] Ryan McDonald, Fernando Pereira, Kiril Ribarov, and Jan Hajič. Non-projective dependency parsing using spanning tree algorithms. In *HLT-EMNLP*, 2005. DOI: 10.3115/1220575.1220641 35, 40

[90] Avihai Mejer and Koby Crammer. Confidence in structured-prediction using confidence-weighted models. In *EMNLP*, 2010. 25

[91] Rada Mihalcea. Co-training and self-training for word sense disambiguation. In *CoNLL*, 2004. 46

[92] Tom Mitchell. The need for bias in learning generalizations. Technical Report CBM-TR-117, Rutgers Computer Science Department, 1980. 5

[93] Makoto Miwa, Sampo Pyysalo, Tadayoshi Hara, and Jun'ichi Tsujii. Evaluating dependency representation for event extraction. In *COLING*, 2010. 7, 80

[94] Yusuke Miyao, Rune Sætre, Kenji Sagae, Takuya Matsuzaki, and Jun'ichi Tsujii. Task-oriented evaluation of syntactic parsers and their representations. In *ACL*, 2008. 7, 80

[95] Raymond Mooney. Comparative experiments on disambiguating word senses. In *EMNLP*, 1996. 19, 24

[96] Alexandru Niculescu-Mizil and Rich Caruana. Predicting good probabilities with supervised learning. In *ICML*, 2005. DOI: 10.1145/1102351.1102430 22, 62

[97] Kamal Nigam, Andrew McCallum, and Tom Mitchell. Semi-supervised text classification using EM. In O. Chapelle, A. Zien, and B. Scholkopf, editors, *Semi-supervised learning*. MIT Press, Boston, US, 2006. 29, 49

[98] Joakim Nivre. Non-projective dependency parsing in expected linear time. In *ACL-IJCNLP*, 2009. DOI: 10.3115/1687878.1687929 39

[99] Joakim Nivre, Johan Hall, Sandra Kübler, Ryan McDonald, Jens Nilsson, Sebastian Riedel, and Deniz Yuret. The CoNLL 2007 Shared Task on Dependency Parsing. In *EMNLP-CoNLL*, 2007. 59

[100] Joakim Nivre, Johan Hall, Jens Nilsson, Atanas Chanev, Gülsen Eryigit, Sandra Kübler, Svetoslav Marinov, and Erwin Marsi. MaltParser: a language-independent system for data-driven dependency parsing. *Natural Language Engineering*, 13(2):95–135, 2007. DOI: 10.1017/S1351324906004505 39

[101] David Palmer and Marti Hearst. Adaptive multilingual sentence boundary disambiguation. *Computational Linguistics*, 23(2):241–269, 1997. 80

[102] Fernando Perez-Cruz. Kullback-Leibler divergence estimation of continuous distributions. In *IEEE International Symposium on Information Theory*, 2008. DOI: 10.1109/ISIT.2008.4595271 14

[103] Slav Petrov, Dipanjan Das, and Ryan McDonald. A universal part-of-speech tagset. CoRR abs/1104.2086, 2011. 6

[104] Slav Petrov and Ryan McDonald. Overview of the 2012 Shared Task on Parsing the Web. In *Notes of the First Workshop on Syntactic Analysis of Non-Canonical Language (SANCL)*, 2012. 59

[105] Barbara Plank and Gertjan van Noord. Effective measures of domain similarity for parsing. In *ACL*, 2011. 30

[106] Hoifung Poon and Pedro Domingos. Unsupervised semantic parsing. In *EMNLP*, 2009. DOI: 10.3115/1699510.1699512 30

[107] Maja Popovic and Hermann Ney. POS-based word reorderings for statistical machine translation. In *LREC*, 2006. 80

[108] Ines Rehbein. Data point selection for self-training. In *The 2nd Workshop on Statistical Parsing of Morphologically Rich Languages, IWPT*, 2011. 44

[109] Roi Reichart and Ari Rappoport. Self-training for enhancement and domain adaptation of statistical parsers trained on small datasets. In *ACL*, 2007. 43, 44

[110] Frank Rosenblatt. The perceptron: a probabilistic model for information storage and organization in the brain. *Psychological Review*, 65(6):386–408, 1958. DOI: 10.1037/h0042519 12, 22

[111] Joseph Le Roux, Jennifer Foster, Joachim Wagner, Rasul Samad Zadeh Kaljahi, and Anton Bryl. DCU-Paris13 systems for the SANCL 2012 Shared Task. In *Notes of the First Workshop on Syntactic Analysis of Non-Canonical Language (SANCL)*, 2012. 59

[112] Kenji Sagae and Andrew Gordon. Clustering words by syntactic similarity improves dependency parsing of predicate-argument structures. In *IWPT*, 2009. DOI: 10.3115/1697236.1697273 50

[113] Kenji Sagae and Alon Lavie. Parser Combination by Reparsing. In *NAACL*, 2006, New York City, NY. 71

[114] Kenji Sagae and Jun'ichi Tsujii. Dependency parsing and domain adaptation with LR models and parser ensembles. In *EMNLP-CoNLL*, 2007. DOI: 10.1007/978-90-481-9352-3_4 46, 59

[115] Kenji Sagae and Jun'ichi Tsujii. Shift-reduce dependency DAG parsing. In *COLING*, 2008. DOI: 10.3115/1599081.1599176 6

[116] Hidetoshi Shimodaira. Improving predictive inference under covariate shift by weighting the log-likelihood function. *Journal of Statistical Planning and Inference*, 90:227–244, 2000. DOI: 10.1016/S0378-3758(00)00115-4 57, 60

[117] David Smith and Jason Eisner. Bootstrapping feature-rich dependency parsers with entropic priors. In *ACL*, 2007. 42

[118] Noah Smith. *Linguistic structure prediction*. Morgan & Claypool, 2011. DOI: 10.2200/S00361ED1V01Y201105HLT013 35

[119] Anders Søgaard. Estimating effect size across datasets. In *NAACL*, 2013. 76

[120] Anders Søgaard. Simple semi-supervised training of part-of-speech taggers. In *ACL*, 2010. 47

[121] Anders Søgaard. Data point selection for cross-language adaptation of dependency parsers. In *ACL*, 2011. 59, 61, 62

[122] Anders Søgaard. Semi-supervised condensed nearest neighbor for part-of-speech tagging. In *ACL*, 2011. 50, 52, 53, 54

[123] Anders Søgaard and Martin Haulrich. Sentence-level instance-weighting for graph-based and transition-based dependency parsing. In *IWPT*, 2011. 30, 61, 62

[124] Anders Søgaard and Anders Johannsen. Robust learning in random subspaces: equipping NLP against OOV effects. In *COLING*, 2012. 70

[125] Anders Søgaard and Barbara Plank. Parsing the web as covariance shift. In *Notes of the First Workshop on Syntactic Analysis of Non-Canonical Language (SANCL)*, 2012. 61, 62

[126] Anders Søgaard and Christian Rishøj. Semi-supervised dependency parsing using generalized tri-training. In *COLING*, 2010. 43, 47

[127] Kathrin Spreyer and Jonas Kuhn. Data-driven dependency parsing of new languages using incomplete and noisy training data. In *CoNLL*, 2009. DOI: 10.3115/1596374.1596380 43

[128] Mark Steedman, Miles Osborne, Anoop Sarkar, Stephen Clark, Rebecca Hwa, Julia Hockenmaier, Paul Ruhlen, Steve Baker, and Jeremiah Crim. Bootstrapping statistical parsers from small datasets. In *EACL*, 2003. DOI: 10.3115/1067807.1067851 43

[129] Ararnaq Subramanya, Slav Petrov, and Fernando Pereira. Efficient graph-based semi-supervised learning of structured tagging models. In *EMNLP*, 2010. 44

[130] Masashi Sugiyama, Satoshi Hara, Paul von Bünau, Taiji Suzuki, Takafumi Kanamori, and Motoaki Kawanabe. Direct density ratio estimation with dimensionality reduction. In *SIAM International Conference on Data Mining*, 2010. 62

[131] Masashi Sugiyama, Shinichi Nakajima, Hisashi Kashima, Paul von Bünau, and Motoaki Kawanabe. Direct importance estimation with model selection and its application to covariate shift adaptation. In *NIPS*, 2007. 61

[132] Qian Sun, Rita Chattopadhyay, Sethuraman Panchanathan, and Jieping Ye. Two-stage weighting framework for multi-source domain adaptation. In *NIPS*, 2011. 5

[133] Charles Sutton, Michael Sindelar, and Andrew McCallum. Reducing weight undertraining in structured discriminative learning. In *NAACL*, 2006. DOI: 10.3115/1220835.1220847 68

[134] Jun Suzuki, Hideki Isozaki, Xavier Carreras, and Michael Collins. An empirical study of semi-supervised structured conditional models for dependency parsing. In *EMNLP*, 2009. DOI: 10.3115/1699571.1699585 42

[135] Joseph Turian, Lev Ratinov, and Yoshua Bengio. Word representations: a simple and general method for semi-supervised learning. In *ACL*, 2010. 50, 67

[136] Wim van den Noortgate and Patrick Onghena. Parametric and nonparametric bootstrap methods for meta-analysis. *Behavior Research Methods*, 37:11–22, 2005. DOI: 10.3758/BF03206394 76

[137] Vladimir Vapnik. *Estimation of dependencies based on empirical data*. Springer, 1982. 12, 25

[138] Kiri Wagstaff. Machine learning that matters. In *ICML*, 2012. 11

[139] Wei Wang and Zhi-Hua Zhou. Analyzing co-training style algorithms. In *ECML*, 2007. DOI: 10.1007/978-3-540-74958-5_42 46

[140] G Wilfong. Nearest neighbor problems. *International Journal of Computational Geometry and Applications*, 2(4):383–416, 1992. 52

[141] David Wolpert. Stacked generalization. *Neural Networks*, 5:241–259, 1992. DOI: 10.1016/S0893-6080(05)80023-1 71

[142] Peng Xu, Jaeho Kang, Michael Ringgaard, and Franz Och. Using a dependency parser to improve SMT for subject-object-verb languages. In *NAACL*, 2009, Boulder, Colorado. DOI: 10.3115/1620754.1620790 80

[143] Hiroyasu Yamada and Yuji Matsumoto. Statistical dependency analysis with support vector machines. In *IWPT*, 2003, Nancy, France. 35

[144] Makoto Yamada, Taiji Suzuki, Takafumi Kanamori, Hirotaka Hachiya, and Masashi Siguyama. Relative density-ratio estimation for robust distribution comparison. In *NIPS*, 2011. 62

[145] Deniz Yuret, Laura Rimell, and Aydin Han. Parser evaluation using textual entailments. *Language Resources and Evaluation*, Published online 31 October 2012, 2012. DOI: 10.1007/s10579-012-9200-5 7, 80

[146] Bianca Zadrozny. Learning and evaluating classifiers under sample selection bias. In *ICML*, 2004. DOI: 10.1145/1015330.1015425 61

[147] Jerry Zhu and Zoubin Ghahramani. Learning from labeled and unlabeled data with label propagation. Technical report, Carnegie Mellon University, 2002. 50

[148] Jerry Zhu and Andrew Goldberg. *Introduction to semi-supervised learning*. Morgan & Claypool, 2009. DOI: 10.2200/S00196ED1V01Y200906AIM006 11, 12, 41, 50

[149] Jerry Zhu, Timothy Rogers, Ruichen Qian, and Chuck Kalish. Humans perform semi-supervised learning too. In *AAAI*, 2009. 41

[150] Jingbo Zhu and Eduard Hovy. Active learning for word sense disambiguation with methods for addressing the class imbalance problem. In *EMNLP-CoNLL*, 2007. 58

Author's Biography

ANDERS SØGAARD

Anders Søgaard was born in Odense, Denmark in 1981. He has worked as a Senior Researcher at the University of Potsdam and is now an Associate Professor at the University of Copenhagen. His research areas include semi-supervised structure prediction, bias correction, and cross-language adaptation of language technology.

Printed in the United States
by Baker & Taylor Publisher Services